THE MARTYRED
ARMENIAN WRITERS
1915 – 1922

AN ANTHOLOGY

HERAND M. MARKARIAN

Second Printing

LIBRA-6 PRODUCTIONS, CONGERS, NY
2015

The Martyred Armenian Writers 1915 -1922

AN ANTHOLOGY

And then all of our dead
Will rise in their graves,
And wait for the arrival of the crimson dawn.
The footsteps of which,
-Believe me, oh, mothers-
I do hear.

Taniel Varoozhan
(Martyred in 1915)

Tonight, the spirits of the dead
In my soul and in my eyes
Are waiting for the dawn to rise.

Siamanto
(Martyred in 1915)

3

L|bra·6

A non-profit organization pursuing Art, Culture and Theater

HERAND M. MARKARIAN
2014
Published in the United States of America by
Libra-6 Productions, Inc.
160 Waters Edge, Congers, NY 10920

Library of Congress Cataloging-in-Publication Data
Markarian, Herand, M.

Martyred Armenian Writers/Herand M. Markarian
Includes biographical references
Translations
Martyred writers
Armenian Poetry
Armenian Language
Armenian History - synopsis
Markarian, Herand, 1938-

TABLE OF CONTENTS

FOREWORD

GENOCIDE IS A CRIME AGAINST HUMANITY

This anthology focuses on thirteen of the most prominent Armenian writers who were martyred during the Armenian Genocide.

The Genocide of Armenians started in April, 1915 in Ottoman Turkey. One and a half million Armenians, out of a total of 2.5 million Armenians living in Ottoman Turkey at the time, were annihilated. At present only about 70,000 Armenians live in Turkey. Of the 2,300 Armenian churches and monasteries, only 32 churches are active in Istanbul today; all the others were demolished or converted to mosques. Of the 2,000 Armenian schools, only 16 schools remain in Istanbul; none in the interior of Turkey.

One can only imagine what the monetary and property loss of the 1.5 million Armenians would be today.

Turkey still denies the Armenian Genocide, although quite a number of prominent Turkish intellectuals and writers have admitted the truth about this historic tragedy.

On the occasion of the one hundredth anniversary of the Armenian Genocide, I hope this anthology gives the reader a sense of appreciation of the literary accomplishments of the Armenian martyred writers. One can only surmise the literature these writers would have created had they not perished during the Genocide. Their loss is humanity's loss.

The translations in this book are original and appear here for the first time.

Herand M. Markarian, Ph.D.
Congers, New York,
January 2015

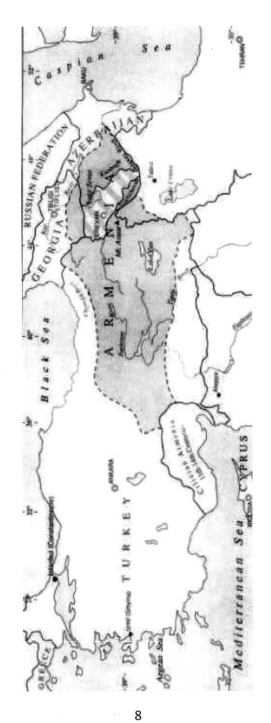

HISTORICAL MAP OF ARMENIA

PART ONE
HISTORICAL HIGHLIGHTS AND ARMENIAN IDENTITY

Armenian identity was molded in the country of Armenia, which was located in Asia Minor, on the eastern border of Greece, then the Roman and later the Byzantine Empires, and the northwest border of the Persian Empire.

In the Book of Genesis the land of Ararat is described as the resting place of Noah's Ark after the "great deluge". The Akkadians called the land "Armani", the Assyrians "Nayiri" and the Greeks called the people of Asia Minor "Armen"'s.

The following dynasties ruled the land, sometimes concurrently, and shaped the Armenian identity: Hayk (2400 BC), the Urartian (883 - 587 BC), Yervantian (Oronthian) (401 - 200 BC), Ardashesian (Artaxias) (189 BC - 1 AD), Arshagoonian, (Arsacids) (66 - 428 AD), Bakradoonian (Bakratid) (885 - 1045 AD), Vasbooragan (908-1021 AD), the Roopenian Principality (1078-1198 AD), Roopenian Kingdom (1198-1219 AD), Hetoomian (1226-1342 AD), Lusinian (1342 - 1375 AD), the Republic of Armenia (1918 - 1920 AD), Soviet Armenia (1920-1991 AD), and the Republic of Armenia (1991 - present).

The largest territory of Armenia was during the reign of king Dikran the Great (Tigranes) (95 - 50 BC).

Armenian history stretches back to the fifth millennium BC when a cohesive culture was shaped on the land. The Nation of Armenia survived throughout the ages because of the following five pivotal factors:

LANGUAGE- Although a "pre-Armenian" language had emerged as early as 2500 BC and the capital city Erebuni (Yerevan) was built in 782 BC by the Urartian King Sarduri the

First, it was King Ardashes I (Artaxias I) who in 189 BC declared Armenian the official language of the state. The Armenian language had developed to a high degree of sophistication to be considered the official language of a state. This was the greatest factor that molded the identity of the Armenian people.

LITERATURE- After the division of Armenia between the Byzantine and Persian Empires in 387 AD, the Armenian alphabet was invented in 405 AD by a monk named St. Mesrob Mashdots, who was aided by Catholicos St. Sahag Bartev and King Vramshabooh. The alphabet became the backbone of survival for the Armenian nation.

The Bible was translated into Armenian from a Greek source; the version used today was completed in 434 AD.

Because of this invention of the Armenian script, there is a massive literature in Armenian which spans over 16 centuries. The Armenian script is still used today.

RELIGION- Armenians were pagans until the fourth century AD. King Drtad III (Tiridates) declared Christianity in 301 AD the religion of the state. Armenia thus became the first Christian nation in world history. St. Gregory the Illuminator was the founder of the Apostolic Church of Armenia which became the cohesive force for survival for the Armenian Nation, especially at times when there was no political leadership. The Armenian Catholicoi used to get ordained in Caesarea, Cappadocia. In 373 AD, King Bab (367-374 AD) stopped that practice thus establishing the independent Apostolic Church of Armenia.

ARCHITECTURE- The first Armenian Church, *Soorp Asdvadsadsin* (Holy Mother of God), was built in 303 AD; it still exists today in Vagharshabad, Armenia. In later years, in spite of Persian (428-645 AD), Arab (639-888 AD), and Seljuk 11th

10

Century rules, a unique Armenian architecture took shape. By the end of the nineteenth century, there were more than 2000 churches and monasteries. One site, where the largest number of churches were built, was the capital city of Ani. The ruins of those churches, some of which remain standing today, are witnesses of a glorious architectural past.

CULTURE- Armenian culture is the very essence of the existence of the Armenian Nation. From pagan times to the present, Armenian songs, dances, rituals, religious hymns, traditional feasts, and theatrical productions have all contributed to the existence of the Armenian culture which reflects the survival of the Armenian Nation.

POLITICAL FACTORS- Political might, successes and failures have contributed to the survival instinct of Armenia. National pride, which is one of the greatest factors for the survival of any nation, is associated with the accomplishment of Dikran II (Tigranes) the Great (95-55 BC), who conquered lands stretching from the Mediterranean north to the Black Sea.

Political failures also have affected the survival of Armenians. Armenians never yielded to their rulers; on the contrary, they adhered to their traditions and to "armenianism." The decline of Armenia began in 1045 AD when the Byzantine Empire conquered Armenia; it was followed by the Seljuks' invasion in 1067 AD. This was a major turning point in the history of Armenia. Armenians sought their survival by migrating to the West. While the majority of Armenians remained on their historic lands, the migrants settled on the north-eastern shores of the Mediterranean Sea, in Cilicia. A new political entity emerged, the Kingdom of Cilicia, which fell to the Memluks of Egypt in 1375 AD.

The years 1050 to 1375 were marked by the creation of major religious literary works. Turkic tribes ransacked Armenia in the 14th century; Ottoman Turkey was established in 1299 AD by Osman Bey of the Oghuz Turkic tribe. Sultan Mehmet II conquered Constantinople in 1453. The Ottomans eliminated all their adversary Turkic tribes from Anatolia, thus becoming the sole controller of the Armenian highlands. The Ottoman Empire and Safavid Persia competed to control Eastern Asia Minor and finally settled their dispute by dividing Armenia in 1639 AD. The eastern part of Armenia, including Yerevan, came under Persian rule. Even under those harsh conditions, the Armenian troubadours composed their most sensitive songs and ballads. In 1603, Shah Abbas of Persia, in order to diminish the support of Armenians to the Ottoman Sultans, forcibly displaced 300,000 Armenians to Persia. This was the beginning of a vibrant Armenian community in Persia

The survival of the Armenians in Ottoman Turkey had a complex path. In 1828, Tsarist Russia defeated Persia and took control of Eastern Armenia. The Tsarist domination lasted nearly one century, until 1918. The Armenians, now under Christian rule, had a relatively relaxed life. Armenian schools were opened and religious freedom was granted. The Republic of Armenia was established in 1918 and lasted for two years. From 1920 to 1991 Armenia was under Soviet domination. Much advancement in literature, architecture and the arts ensued. Soviet Armenia collapsed along with the Soviet Union. Armenia currently is a free and independent country.

Throughout history, the Armenians suffered many atrocities and pogroms; they adapted to the conditions imposed on them by the ruling political powers, but they never gave up their pride and adherence to their past accomplishments.

ARMENIANS IN OTTOMAN TURKEY

The turning point for Armenians living in Asia Minor began when Sultan Mehmet II conquered Constantinople on May 29, 1453 AD.

He crafted a targeted political agenda. In order to dilute the animosity and propaganda about ill-treatment of Christians in Turkey, and to prove to the world that the subjects of Turkey were treated equally. He granted the Christians rites of worship, thus Greeks were granted a Patriarchate.

As for the Armenians, Sultan Mehmet had a different agenda. The highest office of the Armenian Apostolic Church was in Vagharshabad (Etchmiadsin, Armenia), which was controlled by Aq Qoyoonlu Tribe, later by the Shiite Safavid Persia, arch enemy of the Ottomans, who were Sunni Muslims. To have a full control over the Christian Armenians in Turkey, Sultan Mehmet brought Bishop Hovagim from Bursa and established the Armenian Patriarchate of Constantinople in 1461. The Patriarchate was given religious and civil authority over all Armenians living in Ottoman Turkey. Although the Patriarch was elected by the clergy of the Armenian Church, his election was to be approved by the Sultan. In addition to his religious duties, he had the authority to imprison civilians with the approval of the Sultan, which was always granted.

The capital, Constantinople, thus became a safe haven for Christian Armenians, who started flocking into the city, establishing a very influential community.

After the Ottomans were defeated by a combined European army at Vienna in 1683, the Ottoman Empire's expansion was halted.

Further decline of the empire was caused by a series of wars with Russia, which started in 1676 and intermittently

13

lasted almost a century. Russia's successes extended its European frontiers to the Black Sea.

The demise of the Ottoman Empire was clearly on the horizon in the following century. By the 1800s Ottoman Turkey was subjected to European and Russian ambitions from outside and a failing economy, feuds and demands for self-determination and independence from inside. Occupied nations under Ottoman rule such as Hungary, Greece, Libya, Egypt, and the Arab world, one by one rebelled. Ottoman Turkey was described by Tsar Nicholas as "the sick man of Europe".

Responding to external pressures, Sultan Abdulmacid I had to draft a European-style reform edict, the *Tanzimat,* in 1839. This allowed the Armenians to draft their own Armenian National Constitution in 1853, which, in its current version, still guides the national life of Armenians in the Diaspora.

The relatively relaxed political atmosphere in Turkey led to a revitalization of Armenian life. Four hundred and thirty nine schools were established in Constantinople and in the provinces by 1838. Armenian culture was revitalized and the Armenian theater evolved.

This period can be characterized as the era of national awakening. Almost all literary and especially theatrical writings were based on nationalistic themes.

Armenian life in Ottoman Turkey took a downhill turn when Sultan Abdul Hamid II, referred to as The Red Sultan, ascended the throne in 1876. A year later, Russia declared war and Ottoman Turkey was forced to sign the Treaty of San Stefano in 1877 (San Stefano is the present village of Yeshilkoy west of Istanbul). The treaty granted independence to several countries under Ottoman rule but not the Armenians. Article 16 of the Treaty required reforms for the Armenian provinces, which were to be overseen by Russia. Britain opposed the expansion of Russia and managed to organize the Congress of Berlin in the same year. Thus the plight of the Armenians living in Ottoman Turkey was put on a much lower priority level; Article 16 dropped in priority to become Article 61 and European countries were to assure the security of the Armenians. At the Congress of Berlin, Armenians were represented by Patriarch Mgrdich Khrimian. On his return, Khrimian gave his famous "Iron Ladle" speech, where he allegorically talked about a big pot of wheat-dish (*harissa*) placed in a room. "While the representatives of other nations used iron ladles to get their shares of the *harissa*, I had a piece of paper in my hand. When I dipped it in the pot, I couldn't get anything." His reference to an "iron ladle" was a call to self-defense.

Sultan Hamid suspended the Ottoman Empire's constitution and dismissed the parliament, and for the following thirty years became the sole dictator of Turkey.

Hamid's atrocities against the Armenians started in 1894 in the cities of Zeytoon, Sassoon, and Van. In 1895-96 close to 300,000 Armenians were killed; in 1909, 9,000 perished in Adana. The Armenian writers echoed the atrocities in their literary writings.

In 1909, the Young Turk movement restored the constitution and the Ottoman Parliament. The Armenian writers, who had fled Turkey, returned and over the next 6 years produced a massive aesthetic literature, samples of which are given in this book.

These seven years were the calm before the storm.

THE EVOLUTION OF ARMENIAN POETRY

From pagan times, oral renditions (poems, plays, songs, etc.) continued up to the fifth century AD.

What follows is the earliest Armenian poem from pagan times reported by Moves Khorenatsi in the fifth Century AD:

The Song of the Troubadours of Goghtun
The heaven was in travail, the earth was in travail,
The crimson sea was in travail,
The red reed in the crimson sea was in travail,
Smoke burst from the barrel of the reed,
Flames burst from the barrel of the reed,
A blond lad was running through the flame,
His hair was ablaze. His beard was ablaze
And his eyes were blazing suns.

The first sentence written in the Armenian script in 405 AD was the translation of Solomon's verse from the Old Testament (*Proverbs 1:2*)

To know wisdom and advice. To understand words of insight.

The Bible was translated into Armenian from 428 - 430 AD; it was followed by many other translations.

The early poems were spiritual in nature. Here are two of the earliest poems.

Heavenly Father,
Keep Your church unshaken
And keep the worshippers of Thy name
In peace.

Catholicos Sahag Bartev, V Century

16

I am immersed in a multitude of sins,
God of peace, help me.
I tremble by the winds of mischiefs,
God of peace, help me.
I float in the sea of sins,
Oh, Pilot of goodness, save me.

Mesrob Mashdots, V Century

In the tenth century, a quantum leap took place in the Armenian literature. A monk by the name of Krikor Naregatsi (Gregory of Nareg) appeared on the scene. Secluded in the mountains, he set the norms for aesthetic poetry for the ages that followed. His poetry is based on religious themes. However, Naregatsi introduced a luminous use of the Armenian language, inventing new words and thus establishing a super individualistic writing style. His *Madyan Voghperkootyan* (Book of Lamentation) represents a superlative use of the Armenian language. Here is an excerpt:

As I take the road of no-return,
I leave this will to my readers
*   as a reminder of my earthly debts*
So they seek God every day of their lives.
Let this be a cry of lamentation
An everlasting confession in front of You, oh, Omnipotent.
So the writing of my being and the words replacing my soul
*   solicit Your indefinable infinity.*
Accept, oh Lord, the fabric of my words as a petition
From a living and eternal beseecher
To You blessed human God of goodness and Concern.
Amen.

Krikor Naregatsi, X Century

After the fall of the Pakradoonyats (Bagratid) Dynasty in 1045, some Armenians migrated to Cilicia, where a new kingdom was established that lasted until 1375 AD.

The Armenian poetic literature took divergent paths. In Cilicia, literature continued with spiritual themes. The dominant literary figure was Catholicos Nersess Shnorhali (Nersess the Graceful). Being a musician, he introduced a new style of rhyme.

Oh, merciful God
Attend with love the labor of those You created
And send the army of Your angels
To protect us, the weak,
And Guard us from temptations
Of the devil of darkness
So, we praise night and day
Your unsilenced glory.

Nersess Shnorhali, XIII Century, Cilicia

From the twelfth to the thirteenth centuries, rhythm and rhyme, triad, quadric and pentagram forms of stanzas were dominant. These forms, with variations, have persisted to the present. In addition to changes of form, Armenian poetic literature experienced thematic changes as well. Realistic literature emerged in the East, written mainly by troubadours. This was due to the lack of control by the church in the East, which was under siege by Seljuks, Persians, and Ottomans.

The pioneer of this trend was Freeg, a thirteenth-century poet, who dealt with philosophical ideas, human suffering, deprivations, and universal themes.

Vivid love poems appeared in the works of the sixteenth-century free-spirited poet Nahabet Koochag, who introduced

18

octet stanzas; more importantly, however, his poetry is the most daring for the era that he lived in. Here are two examples:

I saw the love of my soul
Dressed-up going to church
I faced her and said,
"Where are you going?
May your prayers never be answered.
If you accept me, I'll be in there too
Praying and pleading
So I could possess your bosom."

***

- I am knocking on your door this dreary night,
Either take me in to your bosom
or tell me to go away.
- How could I tell you to go away?
That's like breaking a child's heart.
Come on in to my bosom and I'll rest you on my chest
make my chest a table to feed from
And my breasts as pillows on your face
I'll button my shirt tightly
So your breath stays with me in my bosom.

Nahabet Koochag, XVI Century

In the 18th century, lyric poetry also continued to flourish and reached a pinnacle of aesthetic presentation in the poems of the great Sayat Nova, who wrote in three languages: Armenian, Georgian, and Turkish. His Armenian is the local dialect of Tbilisi.

Sayat Nova, also a musician, tackled many themes ranging from philosophical to beautiful love poems. He used rhythm and rhyme in superb eloquent coherence. Here are a few samples of his works:

You are of infinite wisdom,
Don't heed the feeble mind.
Don't question us by what you see in your dreams.
I am already seared, don't burn me any more.
If you are bored, don't blame others for it.

***

Your face is shaped like the full moon,
Your hair doesn't need to be braided
It sets without being damped.
That's why people lose their minds when they see you
    enter the court,
      singing and moving gracefully.

***

You are like a precious jewel,
Blessed is he, who will marry you.
Whoever sees you sighs in awe,
Sad is the one who loses you.

***

You are like fire
Your dress is like fire
Which fire shall I endure?

Sayat Nova, XVIII Century

20

WESTERN ARMENIAN LITERATURE
OF THE 19TH CENTURY

In the nineteenth century Armenians lived under two major powers, Ottoman Turkey and Tsarist Russia.

In Turkey, due to the edict of the *Tanzimat* (Reforms) of 1839, political tides relaxed for the Armenians relatively speaking and lasted until the ascension to the throne of Sultan Hamid in 1876.

In Tbilisi, which was under Russian domination, Catholicos Nersess Ashdaragetsi established an Armenian School, named the Nersessian School, which became a hive, where many famous writers and intellectuals studied. In 1874 the Catholicos established the Kevorkian Seminary in Vagharshabad (present-day Etchmiadsin), which continues to operate today.

Two major literary dialects of Armenian emerged during this time period: the Eastern and Western dialects. It should be emphasized that the language is the same. There are very few minor grammatical differences between these two dialects. Armenians in Armenia, Iran, and the former Soviet Union write in and speak the Eastern Dialect; Armenians in the rest of the world write in and speak the Western Dialect. A massive literary output came from both camps.

It is critical to mention that the evolution process of Armenian Literature is a unique phenomenon in the history of the world literature. ALL recorded literatures of the world have evolved in countries, where the written language was the official language of the state. English literature evolved in England; French in France; Italian in Italy, etc., Armenian literature evolved in two non-Armenian countries, where the official languages were Turkish and Russian.

21

This is an amazing accomplishment and most unique phenomenon, indeed! Before Sultan Hamid ascended to the throne in 1876, numerous Armenian newspapers were established which became the media for writers to express their emotions.

Sultan Hamid feared the growth of nationalistic sentiments, and in order to control them, he imposed severe censorship measures on all types of literary, artistic, and informative endeavors of the Armenian papers.

The censorship required the following of all papers:

1-To make their utmost priority reporting on the health of the supreme leader and the economic condition of the country.

2- Not to print any announcement that had not been approved by the Ministry of Education.

3- Not to print long articles; they had to fit the pages of a newspaper. No "continued next issue" was allowed.

4- Not to use dangling punctuation marks that may lead to speculations.

5- Not to criticize the Empire's officials.

6- Not to criticize government officials.

7- Not to use the word *Ermenistan* (Armenia) or any other words that may have relevance to it.

8- Not to inform the public about any assassination attempts committed against rulers of other countries. It also prohibited informing about public uprisings in other nations.

9- Not to interpret these rules.

These severe censorship guidelines forced some Armenian writers to revert to allegorical writing and drove all of them to hide behind pennames. The author Hrant, for example, has used thirteen pennames. The severe censorship lasted until 1909.

After the fall of Sultan Hamid, the seven-year calm before the storm era began, which ended in the catastrophic events of 1915.

Western Armenian literature of the nineteenth century took a parallel path of development to that of European literature. The Armenian literary schools can be divided into the following periods, with some overlaps amongst them.

The Romantic Period- 1850 – 1880

The writers of this period concentrated mainly on awakening the populace to know their rights and history.

The three main genres -- prose, poetry, and theater -- were pursued. There are about seventy writers in this era.

The first generation of this time period included religious writers such as Father Ghevont Alishan in Venice and Bishop Mgrdich Khrimian (later Catholicos of All Armenians). Other writers were: Narbey, Mgrdich Beshigtashlian, Tovmas Terzian, M. Ajemian, Krikor Odian, Nahabed Rroosinian, Bedros Toorian, Dserents, and Srvantsdiants, to name a few. The later generation included Matteos Mamoorian, Srpoohi Dusap (the only woman of the era), Retteos Berberian, Yeghia Demirjibashian, Minas Cheraz, Hagop Baronian, and others.

The writers of this "awakening" period fall under Romanticism; their writings were characterized by intense nationalistic feelings. They were idealistic in nature; at the core of their literature were goodness, honesty, purity, and brotherhood. Their major concern was to illuminate the nation.

Poetry and theatrical writings were abundant. There were novels and chronicles. Bedros Toorian stands out with his poetic talent and expression of personal emotions. He also wrote plays. He died of tuberculosis at the age of 21, leaving behind a respectable literary output.

The Realism Period-   1880 – 1900

The Romantic period came to a halt with the advent of changes in the political climate in Ottoman Turkey. Nationalistic movements, together with the interests of European countries and Russia, led to an entirely new political situation for Armenians.

The severe censorship and the influence of European writers such as Alfonse Dode, Balzac, Flaubert, and Emil Zola shaped a new trend in Armenian literature.

The Realist writers reflected the disastrous struggling and oppression of the Armenians in the provinces and the cities.

The genres that dominated in the era were poetry, chronicles, novella, criticism, and satirical literature. The one genre that suffered was the theater and that was because of the severe censorship, which prohibited the public production of Armenian plays.

The major encourager and "theoretician" of the Realist movement in Armenian Literature was Arpiyar Arpiyarian, who outlined the "creed" of the movement in ten points, which can be summed up as follows: the written language should be understood by everyone; it has to express the reality, the struggle, the aspirations, sorrows and dreams of all classes of the society.

Representatives of the period were Arpiyar Arpiyarian, Krikor Zohrab*, Hrant*, Levon Pashalian, Tlgadintsi*, Yervant Srmakeshkhanlian*, Arshag Chobanian, Yervant Odian, including women writers such as Zabel Asadoor or Sibil (Poetess), Anayis, Mary Svajian, and Zaroohi Kalemkerian.

The Aesthetic Period- 1900-1915

This aesthetic movement started as early as 1900, but it was the year from 1909 to 1915 that marked the most prolific era of

Armenian literary masterpieces. All of the writers mentioned in this anthology produced their masterpieces in these few years almost as an outcry before being silenced. Some of them had started earlier and their works were published outside of Turkey, thus avoiding the severe censorship guidelines of the country. Unfortunately their works did not escape the astute eyes of the Interior Ministry, which recorded all the published works that had "digressed" from the censorship guidelines. These writers later were questioned about their writings and were punished by death sentences.

In these years, Armenian literature took a turn toward aesthetic expressions; poetry reached a linguistic and aesthetic zenith prior to the Armenian Genocide of 1915. The martyred writers in this book were the most influential contributors to Armenian Literature of this era. Adherence to philosophical and ideological principles is at the core of their convictions.

The literature emerging in the provinces had a high aesthetic hue to it. Poetry, with all of its aesthetic, was at the helm of the produced literature. Medsarents, who died at the age of 22, was a major figure. Other names dominating the era were Zartarian*, Siamanto*, Varoozhan*, Indra*, Yessayan, Tekeyan, Shant, Oshagan, Zarian, Zarifian, and others.

Imagery is at the core of the poems, ornamented with old and often newly invented new compound words; each writer literally has his own unique linguistic style. Different structural forms of style are also experimented with during this time. The period remains one of the most amazing bursts of talent; a source of pride not only for Armenians but world literature.

The abyss left behind after the Genocide is the saddest phase in the evolution of Armenian Literature.

* Martyred writers included in this anthology.

25

PART TWO

ACCOUNTS OF THE ARMENIAN GENOCIDE

The decision to exterminate the Armenians in Ottoman Turkey was taken in February 1914 at a highly secretive meeting of the ruling *Ittihad Ve Terreki* Party (Union and Progress Party, or UPP Party). Mehmet Talaat, the Minister of the Interior, and a leading member of UPP, was in charge of implementing the plan.

The Armenian Genocide is one of the most studied and well documented historical events of the 20th century.

Documentations come from different, diverse sources:

a- Eyewitness accounts- There are literally thousands of published accounts, audio and video tapes of eyewitness individuals who went through the experiences of the Armenian Genocide.

b- Politicians' accounts- Almost all of the political figures of nations stationed in Turkey during WWI, ambassadors and consul generals have reported to their respective governments about the mass annihilation of the Armenian people.

c- Historians' accounts- A large number of historians have written scholarly studies unveiling the roots of the Genocide.

d- Reporters' accounts- Pictures, and movies taken by non-Armenian reporters during the atrocities.

e- Missionaries' accounts- The reports of missionaries from different parts of the world are attestations of the atrocities, and

f- The Turkish Government's accounts relating to the attempt of Turkification of Armenian orphans.

Teotig, an Armenian writer and philologist, in his commemorative book lists the names and pictures of 783 Armenian intellectuals arrested in April of 1915, all of whom were killed.

Leslie A. Davis, the American Consul stationed in Turkey said, "A wholesale deportation of this kind in this country means lingering and perhaps even more dreadful death for nearly everyone."

Henry Morgenthau, the US Ambassador to Ottoman Turkey (1913-1916), in a letter addressed to the State Department, wrote,

Secretary of State,
Washington.

858, July 16, 1 p m.

Confidential. Have you received my 841? / Deportation of and excesses against peaceful Armenians is increasing and from harrowing reports of eye witnesses it appears that a campaign of race extermination is in progress under a pretext of reprisal against rebellion.

AMERICAN AMBASSADOR,
Constantinople

"Race extermination" is equivalent to the word "genocide", invented by Raphael Lemkin at the UN conference on Genocide in 1948; Morgenthau most likely would have labeled it as such.

The writers in this book were arrested and executed according to the plan.

CHRONOLOGY OF EVENTS

Very Rev. Krikoris Balakian

Hay Koghkotan (Armenian Golgotha).

April 11, 1915- Saturday evening, and the following Sunday, April 12, 1915, more than 250 intellectuals were detained at *Mehderhane,* the Central Prison of Istanbul, for one day.

April 13, 1915- All detainees were transferred to the port of *Saray Boornoo* or *Gulhane* Gardens. The same day, they were taken by *Shirketi No. 67* vessel to *Haydar Pasha* Station. After two days of waiting, they were led by a train to the interiors of the country.

April 14, 1915- The train, after passing Nicaea, Bardizag (Nicomedia) Izmit, Arslanbeg, and the lake of Sabanchay (Sapancha Golu. HMM) arrived at Eskisheir, the parting station for new directions. The prisoners were divided into two groups. At the station, Ibrahim, from the Central Prison of Constantinople, read a list of 75 names who were to disembark at Eskisheir.

April 14, 1915- The remaing prisoners of the group on the train were directed to Engurl (Ankara. HMM).

April 14, 1915- Evening- The train arrived at Kalayjek. The prisoners weree asked to disembark and were led to a *khan* (a roadside inn).

April 15, 1915- Some of the prisoners from Eskisheir arrived at Senjan Koy leading to Ayash, about a couple of hours away.

The exact dates of executions are not known.

In the provinces, intellectuals, teachers, writers, activists, religious people were detained and killed in the most brutal manner.

28

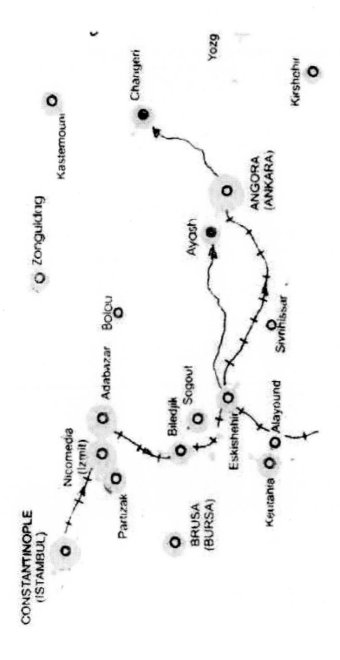

THE ROUTE TO MARTYRDOM

29

PRISON SITES

The writers and intellectuals from Constantinople were detained either in the Ayash prison or exiled to Chankiri; the ones in the Interior were arrested in their own towns and executed.

I- **The Ayash Prison** (60 Km north-west of Ankara).
The following writers were murdered in Ayash Beli:
Melkon Gyoorjian (Hrant)
Smpad Der Ghazariants (Smpad Pyoorad)
Ardashes Harootunian
Roopen Zartarian
Adom Yarjanian (Siamanto)
Kegham Parseghian
Dikran Chogyoorian

II- **The Chankiri Prison,** Chankiri, north-east of Ankara.
The following writers were murdered here:
Taniel Chubookyarian (Taniel Varoozhan)
Roopen Chilingirian (Roopen Sevag)

III- **Kharpert** (Harput., Turkey).
The following writers were murdered here:
Hovhanness Harootunian (Tlgadintsi)
Yervant Srmakeshkhanlian (Yerookhan)

IV- On route to **Dikranagerd** (Diyarbakir, Turkey)
The following writers were murdered here:
Krikor Zohrab
Diran Chrakian (Indra)

THE MARTYRDOM OF
TANIEL VAROOZHAN AND ROOPEN SEVAG

By Michael Shamdanjian
(An Exiled Companion)

There were 150 of us when we arrived at the town of *Changhuru* (Chankiri, a town north east of Ankara. HMM).

Thirty persons were allowed to return to Constantinople. Out of the remaining 120, today only 15 persons have survived.

Two convoys of 50 persons each were exiled to the desert of Der El Zor. The first group's members were more of the muscular type; why this choice? We couldn't comprehend. Only two people out of the exiled 100 survived: a Protestant by the name of Baronian and Aram Andonian, who had a broken foot and was left behind. (Andonian later wrote his very important memoirs about their ordeal. HMM).

Roopen Sevag, being a physician, had tended to the daughter of Arabaju Bashy Ismail. The latter suggested to Sevag to convert to Islam and marry his daughter. Sevag refused.

In the following days, Mr. Jemal Oghuz, the representative of the Union and Progress Party, read a list compiled of those who were to be pardoned. Varoozhan's and Sevag's names were not on that list. The latter two immediately telegraphed Constantinople seeking help.

On August 26, 1915, a coach stopped by our door. Taniel Varoozhan, Roopen Sevag, and their three friends (Onnig Mazmanian, Vahan Kehyaian, Artin Agha. HMM) were led into it. We accompanied them to the town's limit and bid farewell. Twelve hours later the news of their martyrdom reached us. Ironically twenty four hours later, Sevag's wife (an Austrian citizen. HMM) had secured the release of Sevag.

We came across Hassan, the coachman, who was a resident of Chankiri and had accompanied the exiled five.

This is what he told us, *'The night before the incident, a horseman came and ordered me to take care of his horse; he went to the house, where the party members were holding their meetings for a couple of days.*

'In the morning of August 24, before sunrise, another man came and ordered me to go about a quarter hour outside of the village and wait for the police. There was another coach there. There were a policeman and five gentlemen. One of them was a young man with a black beard and bright eyes (Sevag, HMM.) Their hands were tied. They had a worried look. The policeman ordered them to come to my coach. He ordered us to take off toward Tyooney village.

'We rode about an hour. We arrived at a bend in the road, and then the same man, who had visited me the night before, appeared. He crossed our path and started circling around the coach. Half way to Tyooney, the same man appeared and dismounted from his horse. He held the bridle and guided the coach off the road to a down-sloping ditch. I jumped off the coach, so did the policeman; we thought we were going to be robbed. At the same time, a clerk from the police headquarters came and respectfully bowed his head to the man. At that moment four fully armed men appeared.

'The official, who seemed to be the head of the four, signaled them. The armed men tied the prisoners' and our hands and feet and took the five gentlemen toward the ditch. Because their hands were tied, the policemen started searching the gentlemen for their possessions. They took their money and cigarettes. The policeman whispered something to the leader of the bandits, seemingly to have a share of the loot. After that they left. They untied me and ordered me to go back to town.

They ordered the gentlemen to follow the bandits. I was watching from a distance to see where were they being taken. They passed the valley to the other side. Their leader said something, which I didn't hear; but the bandits stormed at the gentlemen; they stripped them to bare nakedness. They tied them to trees. They couldn't defend themselves. The group took out their daggers and began beheading them in a calm manner. Their screeches of their calls still haunt me...'

THE MARTYRDOM OF
INDRA (DIRAN CHRAKIAN)

By Ohan Bedigian
(An exiled Companion)

At the end of February 1921, Chrakian, Kaspar, and Hovsep Kolaji were detained being accused of sabotage activities, namely, spreading Christianity Sabbatarianism (Seventh-Day Adventism) in Ottoman Turkey. Kaspar and Hovsep were condemned to death; Chrakian was exiled on April 14 to Diyarbakir in chains. He was taken to Nide'. On May 1, along with 28 others, he was "taken on the road"... the group was not allowed to rent an oxcart. Chrakian was separated from the group and was sent to Caesarea to join other exiled individuals from Bilejig. The next morning we were robbed.

We arrived at the town of Gemergi, where there were twenty Armenian women and four or five converted Armenians.

We were taken from Caesarea to Sivas, where we arrived in ten days. We remained in Sivas for two days, where we got support from the Armenians still living there.

In the town of Eskisheir, near Malatya, we came across women in Turkish dresses, who, realizing that we were Armenians, offered us bread.

Under brutal conditions of beating and torture, we arrived at *Kharpert* (Harput). The local Armenians found out about the exiled and sent a delegation to investigate the situation. Chrakian handed them a letter addressed to Bishop Kiyood, the Primate. Moments later, a woman visited us and handed us ten Ottoman gold coins.

We then were taken to Diyarbakir. After a long wait, we finally were successful in buying fifteen loaves of bread with one gold coin. Chrakian was totally distraught and sick. He could hardly walk. The news was delivered to the police chief, who came and lashed Chrakian saying, "Don't desecrate this site by dying here; go and do whatever you want on the road." We carried him on our backs up until the Tigris River. After crossing the river, Chrakian was ill with fever, started hallucinating and went mad. He held his shoes in his hands and ran to the river and jumped in. We saved him with difficulty.

The next morning on June 6 we set out on the road again. Realizing that we couldn't carry Chrakian anymore, we asked the police chief to carry him on his horse. After much negotiation, the police chief agreed to do that for two gold pieces. Where would we get the money? After further negotiation, the police chief agreed to take Chrakian's coat and trousers.

Chrakian was so weak that he couldn't ride the horse. Three hours later we arrived at a brook. We took him down and laid him on the floor. He barely rested a moment, turned to us and wished us love and unity, and died.

PART THREE

BIOGRAPHIES AND LITERARY WORKS
OF
THE MARTYRED ARMENIAN WRITERS

HRANT

(Melkon Gyoorjian)

1859 -1915

HRANT
(Melkon Gyoorjian)
1859 -1915

"Our most precious possessions are our script and our books."

Hrant

HRANT (Melkon Gyoorjian)
1859 - 1915

BIOGRAPHY- Melkon Gyoorjian (pen name Hrant) was born in the village of Havav, Palou Province, Ottoman Turkey. He attended the town's elementary school. The family moved to Constantinople, where he attended the Uskudar Lyceum until 1875 and then the *Soorp Khach* (Holy Cross) high school. After graduation in 1878, he taught Armenian literature and history at the *Getronagan* (Central) high school, and *Noonian-Vartoohian* schools. He was accused in 1893 of being a revolutionary and was arrested for a month. He barely escaped Sultan Hamid's massacres of 1896, and moved to Varna, Bulgaria, where he and Miss Armenoohi Minassian established the *Ardsroonian* School (named after the famous writer Krikor Ardsrooni, whom he admired), and a school for children of emigrant families. He returned to Constantinople in 1898 and was immediately arrested and exiled to *Kastemooni*, a town near the Black Sea, where he stayed for ten years teaching in Armenian schools. In 1909, when the new constitution was adopted, he returned to Constantinople and went back to teaching. In 1909 he was elected a delegate to the Armenian Church Assembly in Etchmiadsin.

He was arrested along with 250 intellectuals in Constantinople on April 12, 1915 and was taken to *Ayash* Prison. He was martyred in 1915.

LITERARY ACOMPLISHMENTS- Although he began writing in 1883, his presence in the literary circles was not felt until 1888, when he became a regular contributor to the *Masis* weekly newspaper. All of his literary writings appeared in the following newspapers in Constantinople: *Masis, Hairenik,* and *Azadamard.*

Novels- *Puzantion* (The Byzantium), *Yergoonk* (The Labor), *Dsaghig yev Sharzhoom* (Flower and Movement), *Bantookhti* Gyanken* (From the Life of a Migrant), 1888, *Badizhuh* (The Punishment), 1892, *Gyanki Muh Kaykayoomuh* (The Shattering of a Life), 1893, *Yergoo Vermagi Dag* (Under Two Covers), 1895, *Teghin Tooghter* (Yellow Papers), 1895, *Khanin Yergrord Harguh* (The Second Floor of the Inn), 1913, *Arrants Piloni Kahanan* (The Priest Without a Cloak), 1913, *Keghi Namagner* (Letters from the Village), *Khaneroon Mech Bekar guh Bagser?* (Was there a shortage of Bachelors in the Inns?).

Essays- *Mesrob yev Sahag Hay Nshanakreroo Badmootyoonuh* (The History of Armenian scripts by Mesrob and Sahag).

Translations- "The Life of Christ" by Renan; "What do Women Think of Their Husbands" {author unknown, HMM}, *Krapari Lezoo* (Classical Armenian – a textbook).

PENNAMES: Avo, Arnold, Bondatsi, G.M., Hrant, M.G., M.S.G., Ooghevor (The Voyager), Shahen, Shavasp, Tughtagits (Correspondent), Tughtagits ee Bondos (Correspondent in Bondos), Tughtagits Bondosi (The Correspondent of Bondos), and Vartkes.

LITERARY CHARACTERISTICS- His focus was the lives of *bantookht* Armenians. His deep concern for the Armenian villager, who left his family and home for the city, in search of a better life for his family, became the overriding theme in all of his writings. He writes about their complicated lives, their struggles, their hopes and aspirations in this strange environment. He visits the inns that the *bantookhts* had chosen as home and observes their living conditions. He talks to them attempting to alleviate their worries and concerns. He is a keen observer of the challenges of this society and vividly describes the conflicts therein.

In Western Armenian literature, Hrant is the only writer who really understood the deleterious effect of emigration on society and, in addition to his writings; he attempted to discourage emigration by lecturing extensively against it.

His language is simple and his prose is clear. His sensitivity and sincerity touch the reader and make his writing a sought after source of Armenian prose.

He started as a chronicle writer for newspapers, but through his superb treatment of the sentiments of *bantookhts** and the usage of simple language, he ascended to literary heights.

The literary critic Hagop Oshagan states, "Hrant found the golden artery of his people's sentiments. His literature is endowed with honesty and tender emotionalism."

Bantookht- Men who have temporarily moved to cities and countries seeking work to support their families; they intend to go back one day. The word also connotes forcibly expelled or exiled. Other homonyms are *Nzhteh* (pilgrim), *vdaranti* (exiled, deported), *darakir* (banished, expatriated), *asdantagan* (vagabond), and in colloquial Armenian borrowed from Arabic, *Gharib* (estranged). Due to the fact that the word embodies so many meanings, we decided to use the Armenian word, thus keeping its authenticity.

THE MEMORIAL EIGHTH DAY

A.

Smallpox had infected the house of a wealthy family and claimed the life of the most handsome youngest male member. The hierarchies of the church ordered an elaborate burial ceremony. To give it an air of royalty, they ordered eight to nine year old pupils to carry the coffin with their little hands; of course these children should be from poor families.

The funeral procession moved along with twelve little children carrying the coffin, followed by an entourage of dignified clergy. The lady of the house, with tears in her eyes, was watching her beloved son's funeral procession. I doubt if she realized that she had placed Death in the palms of the little pall bearers. To her, most important was that nothing would be missing from the grandeur of the funeral - members of the clergy, crosses, hymns, and of course the newly added little coffin-bearers. There was even a bishop with a staff in his hand marching with the clergy. A real pompous mourning ceremony...

It was cold! A cold wind was blowing down the street. The little coffin-bearers, adjacent to Death, felt the severity of the weather. The procession went forth with the air of artificial grandeur by the swaying clergy.

B.

That night the grieving mother was content that she had given her child everything she could. It did not occur to her how, in that cold weather, the coffin-bearing children had returned to their mothers. Of course that was unimportant; after all, they were children of the poor.

42

But the children had been in contact with the deadly disease, especially the youngest boy. He had gone home shivering from the cold. His body was aching. His mother thought that it was just a simple cold. She didn't know what her son had done that day.

In the next and following days the child didn't improve; his fever progressed and the trembling persisted. The family could not afford a doctor - they did not have the money - all they could do was to invite the priest to say a prayer for the child and hope for a miracle.

The mother sat by her son's bed and watched him all night long. In the morning when she touched her son's forehead the child had died and she realized it was smallpox. The coffin-bearer was no longer here.

Then came the funeral preparations. The church bell didn't toll. The boy's father was the only one directly walking behind the coffin. A priest was also present, but was careful to be a measured distance from the coffin. A short prayer and the coffin was placed to rest in a little ditch for a grave.

The next day, as the mother was going through the little boy's belongings, she found 50 para (the smallest denomination of Turkish coins) in his pocket. She surmised that this was money her son had received for carrying the coffin - he had walked beside Death.

The eighth day fell on the day before New Year. The mother remembered that last year she had held her child's hand and gone to church, where the young boy played with his friends.

Now, the eighth day was dark, an eternally dark night... there were to be no more mornings, no more New Year, nor sun on the lost horizon.

LIVES OF *BANTOOKHTS*

A.

There are no vacant rooms in the inns.

New, young people have come from all over: from every town and city.

Glancing at them one sees that the majority are in their teens, ranging in age from 14-16. They are dressed pathetically with shabby, well-worn shoes that have survived walking 15-29 days through valleys and mountains to reach Constantinople.

Who cares about these destitute people? The majority are orphans, who had hoped to find a distant relative or a neighbor in the city.

They wait for days and months. Having arrived with borrowed money for their trips, the youngsters are away from their homes and relatives and are deprived of the love and caring of their loving families.

The mothers naively believed that the moment their sons reached Constantinople, they would send money back home and all their worries would be solved.

Just two months after the departure of her son, a mother writes, "Son, send us money by the next post service. You know, I borrowed money to send you to Bolis (Constantinople)."

The inns are flooded with letters of this kind. Young souls read them and, not being able to do anything, become emotionally upset.

One day, I don't remember when, I entered a room in the inn; a distressed young man named Mardig was leaning on his bed with his hand on his head.

What's bothering you? I asked.

Nothing!

Later I learned that his mother had sent him a letter in which she had mentioned their growing debt.

The son not only didn't have a job, but he was not even being trained for one. He was one of many young boys whose lives were nothing but constant struggle for their age. Some might succeed, but you know how? They would work 12 hours a day carrying heavy loads up and down ladders. I have seen many of these boys collapse under their burdens.

Mardig's story is similar to so many.

He had now been in Bolis for two years and was sixteen years old. His father, upon his return home, had been lost in the mountains of *Garin* (Erzurum) and thus had no grave. His mother, Takoohi, was left with four children. She decided to send Mardig, then fourteen years of age, to Bolis.

The fourteen year old boy is here with his father's debt of fifty gold coins hanging like a chain from his neck. Added to that is the expectation of his home, looking to him for help.

We found this boy when he was fourteen years old and took him home with us, saving him from being beaten by his bosses.

At age sixteen he decided to go to work – the usual age for that kind of labor.

One evening I came home and didn't find him. He had gone to the inn.

Pride had driven him there to earn money in a responsible manner.

One Sunday he visited us; he was in rags and worn-out shoes. What had he earned? Only seventy-five *Tahegan* in forty days of work. He was struggling to make it a hundred, the equivalent of a gold coin in order to send it home. He had deprived himself of all pleasure.

Mardig's life was that of many like him; at least this one was saved from the torment of the insults by bosses.

B.

Autumn is the only season where *bantookhts* experience both happiness and sorrow. Autumn is the season of longing and hope. Before the leaves turn yellow, steamships ferry our brothers to the shores of Samson and Trabzon. The *bantookht* is so excited to set foot again on shores of the land he left one beautiful spring many years ago. He turns west and looks at the city where he worked many years ago.

He is truly a new man.

How many days does it take to shed the weight of the years he spent patiently, without complaint, in the darkness of the inns in Constantinople? And now, in these few short days, he has the heavy burden of catching up with the times lost: love of home, of parents, of family, and love of the mountains and the valleys. These emotions come to life as unbearable pain in the *bantookhts'* chest. - What? Does the *bantookht* have a heart?

It takes only a day to shed the troubles of the Black Sea. A day later, even before the sun rises, caravans go forth.

Along the way, our *bantookht* sees St. Peter's brook, which he had crossed years ago. He sees the little hill, from where he saw the Black Sea for the first time -that blue sea- lying under a blue sky.

To get to their final destinations, some of them have to travel for a month, others for fifteen days.

Have you seen the highlands of Derseem, the valleys and mountains of Greater Hayk (Western Armenia)? The peaks of these mountains pierce the clouds and the depth of the valleys approach Hell. It takes a day to climb these heights and a day to descend walking over rocks and thorns.

The East is like a compass that guides the path of the *bantookhts'* journey to fulfill their longing. The sky and the climate are not kind. It is cold, the ground is muddy; snow and

46

rain are constant companions. The travelers have no protection from these elements; they are totally drenched. There are elderly, too. The last time Brother Boghos crossed these lands he was 65 years old. Leaning upon his cane he had climbed the rugged mountains of Derseem. He had more faith than Moses; he had reached the land of his ancestors and his home. At nights he had to nestle under tree branches and at times found shelter in stables. Those heartless owners would not even give him a spot next to their oxen. In the morning, it was walking again... walk and walk... and one day the difficult road would end; the caravan ascends to the top of the mountains and from thereon it is downhill just as the last moments of the day pass under the hands of the clock.

The village appears at a distance with its chimneys smoking. A long sigh emits from exhausted lungs, "Blessed is the Lord." Then the vineyards appear, as does the dome of the church and the monastery that protects our villages. Here the walnut tree stands with its bare branches extending into the air. The white poplar tree sways in the wind and in the cemetery; the crosses spread their black arms over the white snow, and there, the stone chapels of St. Giragos, Lady Varrvarr, St. Hagop, and St. Sarkis that encircle the village.

Questions swarm in the minds of the *bantookhts*. One anxiously wonders, will he be able to see all those whose names were mentioned in the letters sent to him, realizing full well that most of the time, those names were mentioned to deceive him? Another thinks, will he find his beloved baby he left in the crib has grown and is a mature man? Yet a third ponders, will he find his young wife, with whom he spent four months only?

"Don't be afraid my friend, with God's help everyone is alive and well." -Poor souls! - That's all they have - "dependence on

God." They are poor, they are lost, and they have nothing but sorrow and misery.

These thoughts are barely lost in the air, when a burst of gunshots is heard in the valley. A bright flame, like a rainbow, arches over the village east to west. The entire village is happy and excited- "The boys have returned."

Everyone is about. Grandpas and grandmas are excited. The crowd runs to greet the returning boys: there's someone's sister, another's brother, a baby and his mother... but missing is the wife... village tradition forbids her to greet her husband in public. Is it at all possible to explain the deep-felt happiness in the embrace of the returnees and the greeters? They tell someone, "Here's your child." They tell another, "Here's your brother." God only knows the many times they tell a mother "Here's your son," a son who had left as a teenager and now has returned a full grown brave adult with a curved mustache. And, there, alone, a hunchbacked elder is walking... he, too, in a sense is a *bantookht*.

Zumo, Kamo, Zolo, Dule, Mooro have not forgotten their masters, and each runs excitedly to his master, rubbing against his legs while curling his tail.

"Garo, dear, isn't there someone to greet you? Where are your father, mother?"

A mother-in-law to be comes to greet her future son-in-law; she endured the agony of the emigration and she displays an obvious pride.

Zemo, Garo's loyal dog, whom Garo cared for as a puppy, comes and jumps on his master.

With many questions on his mind, wiping the tears of happiness, Garo enters his home. There are his parents. His grey-haired elderly father, who even with his cane is barely able to reach the door and greet his only son. His mother, also old, is more mobile. She is able to cook and help her husband.

Oh! If you could only see the tears of happiness coming from his father's dried eyes rolling down into the wrinkles of his aged cheeks and onto his grey beard. If you could only see his frail mother hugging her son, an expression of her sentiments in the last barren years of her life. The lanterns are glowing, as is everyone's heart, and the logs crackle in the fireplace. At this time, there are no worries; everything has come to pass. There are no wanderers and there are no more heartache.

Let these people enjoy their beautiful moments; let us knock on other doors.

Here is another old man. Let us ask him, why are you upset? Let us ask this young woman, why are you sad?

Oh! How many of the *bantookhts* had written that they were to come home in the autumn, but actually few returned. Now that the last of returnees has arrived and winter is here, all hopes for others to return are lost. The old man does not think that he'll survive the winter. The young wife has dashed her hopes. Do you see those black pages, the death notices that exchange hands in awe and no one attempts anymore to send letters to those addresses? Do you know what they say? "Mano was buried here," "Zakar died in Trabzon," "Ohan and Ohanness, who were only 45 and 18, are here no more." Sad, sad events.

Bear with me and let us read one of those letters that is still moist from tears that were shed.

"Many greetings to my mother Mako (Markrid), my brother Tate', brides, boys and babies, sisters, and to all who inquire about us." Ago, servant of Christ.

"Although I can't really write, but it is God's will for me to try. This autumn, Mano was coughing heavily. One day he had

49

travelled a great distance seeking a job. That night, on his way back, it rained and he, soaking wet, coughed a lot. In the morning I woke him up to go to work; he didn't want to get up. I asked, 'What is it, Mano?' He said, 'My chest hurts; I have no strength.'

"Two days later, we begged him to go to *Soorp Prgich* (Holy Savior) Hospital. Reluctantly, he agreed. At night when I came home, I learned that Mano had walked to the hospital. A day later, Sunday, I went to see him. He was lying in a bed with bottles of medicine lined up on the side table. When he saw me, he laughed. I stayed for an hour and left. I secretly gave a gold coin to the nurse who was circling me and asked her, 'In the name of God, please look after him; he has a wife and children.' I walked back to our inn, but my heart was left behind.

"That night, I dreamt of Mano. He had fully recovered and without a cough and appeared quite healthy, just as before. He was dressed in his wedding attire. 'Where are you going, Mano?' I asked. He didn't answer. He pointed to the heavens. I awakened in fear. The sun had not yet risen. It was not a good dream. I went to the café without saying a thing to anyone.

"I was sad. The sun rose. I was told someone was asking for me. I understood what had happened; Mano was no more.

"Two of us went to see him. He was covered in shrouds. We took him to the cemetery. God bless our *bantookht* priest. With his trembling voice he recited the entire burial rites. He blessed the grave with the cross and said, 'May my blessing be eternal.'

"Dear Mother, had he recovered a little bit to endure the harsh travel, I would have sent him home so he could be buried next to my father in our village cemetery; at least you could have burned incense every Saturday night.

"What to do? Such is God's will, Mom. May you be well."

Many such letters are received by villagers. When night falls and before the lights go out, the hope in many anxious hearts will be lost forever. Someone leaves behind young orphans and a young widowed wife; others leave mothers, elderly fathers, and a home... This is what happened when they first left home.

The *bantookhts* also have home, mourners, and friends who share their happy moments.

Isn't this strange?

C.

We were walking uphill, when I heard a soft voice- I turned. "Twenty Para, please, I haven't had anything to eat today," claimed the voice. He was one of our *bantookhts*. His emaciated face had the redness of starvation. He had recognized me.

I recognized him too, though he was hidden under worn-out clothes and the build of old age. He was Master Arrakel, who had worked for twenty five years as a mason. A humble man, now in his elder years, was begging for a mere twenty Para. It should be said that these people don't know how to beg.

Some time came to pass, when I heard that his comrades had collected enough funds and were able to send the old man back home. Now he lives where he was born and he'll stay there; he does not have to fear migrating ever.

The roads of migration for our countrymen from Trabzon, Samsun, and Crassus are terminated, when old, starving and incapable men are sent home with collected "mercy" money. They become protectors of their homes, that is, if the elderly are worth anything.

I don't remember where I have read that there is an island somewhere, when the elderly realize that their lives are worthless, they commit suicide. It is the same with *bantookhts*. Sadly, the only thing accomplished is that cemeteries become vital places.

TLGADINTSI

(Hovhanness Harootunian)

(1860 – 1915)

"When nations abandon their traditions, that's when real death begins."

Tlgadintsi

TLGADINTSI (Hovhanness Harootunian)
1860 -1915

BIOGRAPHY- Tlgadintsi was born in the village of Tlgadin (Khoylu, Turkey) in the region of Kharpert (Harput), Western Armenia (current Turkey). He lost his father at an early age. Through his mother's efforts, he attended the local school and then the *Smpadian* School in Kharpert. After graduation he worked as a clerk at the Diocese in Kharpert. From 1884 on, he taught in the local schools in Kughi and Palou. In 1897 he founded the Central National School of Kharpert and functioned as its principal until the end of his life. One of his most famous students was the writer Roopen Zartarian, who is written about in this anthology.

In 1903 he was accused of spreading nationalistic views and was imprisoned for almost a year; after his release, he returned to teaching.

He never went to Constantinople; he lived his entire life in the provinces.

In 1915, during the mass extermination of Armenian intellectuals, he hid in a Turkish friend's house, but was soon discovered, exiled, and killed along with many other intellectuals from the same area in the village of Arek, near Kharpert.

LITERARY ACCOMPLISHMENTS- His early writings appeared in the 1880's in the Constantinople newspapers *Masis* and *Arevelk* (East).

His literary contributions are in the following genres:

Chronicles- These are about events, people, and the terrible economic conditions that were present in the provinces.

Novels- *Heen Havadkuh* (The Old Belief), 1895, *Kulkhoot Choor Tir* (Pour Water on Your Head), 1896, *Aykiyis Pushenin* (The Thorn Bush in My Garden), 1898, *Verchin Deghuh* (The Last Place), 1900, *Jakhragin Arrachkuh* (In Front of the Spinning Wheel), 1900, *Bidsagneroon Tsaynuh* (The Sound of Wasps), 1907, and *Kavat Muh Miyan* (Just a Cup), 1907.

Plays- He is known to have written thirteen plays, of which some are titled: *"Enti Temen" (*From the Other Side), 1902, *"Gdaguh"* (the Will), 1911, *"Vor Megoon Yedeven"* (Who to Follow?), *"Zalum Dughan" (*The Naughty Boy), *"Tebi Ardasahman"* (Going Abroad); *Jamportn oo Gametsoghneruh* (The Traveler and the Well Wishers).

He has also written several poems.

PENNAMES- H. H., T., Parrnag, Tlgad, and Tlgadintsi.

LITERARY CHARACTERISTICS- Tlgadintsi's novels are a reflection of his times. He has written about the various tragedies following the 1896 Hamidian massacres, describing helpless, abandoned people and the orphans. He writes about life in the villages to create awareness in city dwellers. In his letters from the village he says, "The pain of the villages is evident in many ways. You may say this is their life; they are accustomed to it. Their struggle has made them strong like bones, which have then turned into iron. Our neighbors, the snakes and deer, are happier than us."

Tlgadintsi describes the awful conditions of the Armenians living in Ottoman Turkey. His writings are in rural dialect, but in a refined artistic manner and with a sense of humor and optimism. He writes, "We have the Armenian alphabet, and so we are eternal, we will never die or disappear."

MY LUCK

I came and I'll leave with shattered dreams
With an empty heart and exhausted soul
Empty like a straw, deprived of its sap,
Bare like a vine, deprived of its leaves. I looked at the
Mountain, I saw only snow,
And shreds of clouds beyond the mountains,
Above them, I saw a dark sky only,
While beneath it all lay a deserted land.
They say there are more than one sun
That make the world fertile.
Where are the suns? Where are they hiding?
I haven't seen even a single ray now.
Oh, poor, poor, unlucky Tlgadintsi,
Didn't see a ray, not on the ground nor up in the sky.

***

Don't look at me, my sweet love,
Don't look at me with your beautiful eyes,
When you leave your house, don't look at me.
For I am not a stone that could resist
The beautiful reflection of your eyes.

THE JUDGMENT OF THE BIRDS

One day, the good Lord found Himself amazed at the sparrows - the little grey creatures, colored like the earth- that had travelled all the way from Earth to His kingdom.

One of the sparrows had the courage to come forth and relate their complaint, thus surprising the leader of the birds, the hawk.

Before becoming emotional, the Creator of the heavens and earth said, "Birds, do you know how I created you? When I was creating the great things, I brushed off the remaining earth on my hands and that's how you came to be. As I did for man, ants, and all creatures, I gave you many good things: an abundance of land to feed from, a space in the tallest buildings for you to build your nests... What else do you want? And let me tell you, humans have to struggle for their food, but you can eat without even sowing seeds. You can eat anything man leaves on the streets. You have insects and grasshoppers to eat. What else do you want?"

One of the birds came forward and said, "Lord, we have a different request."

-"Be short and to the point. Are you going to point out mistakes I have done?"

- "Lord, have mercy; it is nothing like that."

- "Fine, I am listening."

- "We have a complaint about the priest in our village. The other day he acted in a manner that froze us in astonishment."

- "The priest of your village? But I have known him to be a good shepherd."

- "We always felt that way too..."

- "And..."

-"The other night, he was walking toward the church carrying his cross. We were gathering the crumbs that were falling off a cart – and having our evening meal. He took a stone and threw it at us."

- "What happened with that stone?"

- "It broke the wing of one of our little birds. The poor bird couldn't fly anymore. It lay there and by now is surely dead."

- "Oh, that is bad, indeed..."

- "Bad and really sad, Lord. That poor soul was the only one remaining in his family. There were three: one disappeared mysteriously, the other attempted to fly prematurely and died, and the third, a real fine bird, died by the hand of the priest in front of the church. Have pity on us, Lord. We believe that the good Lord is also concerned about us."

- "Shall I sever his hand? I can give an order for lightning to strike and that will be instantly accomplished."

- "No, Lord, we wouldn't want that."

- "Shall I blind him? I can order eagles to gouge out his eyes and make a pouch for insects to live in."

- "That will be worse, Lord."

- "Why?"

- "A blind man can't see; he could crush lives and other precious things under his feet. A blind man could very easily claim innocence."

- "It seems you know what you want. Tell me!"

- "Lord, we beseech you to send the barber of the village and have him shave the priest's beard."

- "How would that solve the problem?"

- "Up until now, whenever we saw a layman, we would fly away from him, fearing he might harm us. Now that we have been betrayed by the bearded, ordained man, we ask you to remove that identifying appendage. A punishment like that will reaffirm our faith that a priest is God's person, always a good and holy person who would not even harm an ant. That's all we want."

The good Lord listened to the birds' request and ordered the village barber to shave the priest's beard.

Now, whenever birds see a shaven man, they fly away hurriedly.

The birds joyfully chirping returned to earth, thinking there is a kind God in the Heavens.

Lucky birds!

TELL ME WHAT HAS HAPPENED

(To the Memory of My Mother)
(Excerpt)

It's been five or six months that I have not seen her. But I have not forgotten her; I remember every syllable of her sweet words and even the essence of her prayer. She tried to teach it to my little son, Zaven, and would end it with a lovely fairy-tale.

I also remember my mother's prayer along with her quiet and silent goodness.

"Good morning, God, good morning, Christ of goodness. Please take away evil and give us goodness. Grant peace to the world and conciliate the kings. Thy will is everything, heavenly God. Give us short nights and long days, small sorrows and much laughter, little anxiety and much tranquility, short periods of impoverishment and prolonged periods of joy. You are omnipotent. You can bestow anything. Mountains, Heavens and Earth tremble in awe of Your might.

"Good morning, God, Christ of goodness. I come to You as sacrifice for your Light. I come to You with complete belief in You. I subject myself to You in total worship. Please, God, grant health to my children and success in their careers. Don't let the deprived be needy and please, Lord, grant me a peaceful death and a flourishing heavenly life. Heavenly Father, don't judge us by our trespasses and don't punish us for our sins. Please accept our prayers for the souls of our departed. We have put our trust in You. Oh, Lord of light and goodness..." etc. etc...

At the end she would say The Lord's Prayer and then make the sign of the cross.

When she returned from church services, she would gather the little ones around her as her audience. I had grown tired of listening to her stories about her dreams the night before. She had a special way of telling and interpreting her dreams, which she claimed was based on her personal experiences. She sincerely believed that dreams dreamt at dawn would, somehow, sooner or later, come true. That is what she would say every day. Slowly, I became convinced, too. I began following the happenings of the day to see if something really had incited them. Secretly, I would look at her face in the morning. If I noticed a smile, it meant that she had had a good dream the night before... Then I would be off to work feeling more at ease... otherwise I would not say a word.

All of us in the household were fascinated with her interpretation of her dreams. She would say, "Anyone of us riding a red horse will have good luck." Salt... meant pain; oil spilled on a dress... bad luck; baking white bread... immediate success; sermon and priest... conflict, turmoil in the house, wedding; drum roll... definite death; tooth being pulled... death of a relative; a tree in the vineyard, flowers and crystal waters... good dreams... etc...

It was interesting, but I don't know when she left the village to live in the city. Even after so many years, village life remained the foundation of her life. The village with its trees; the village with its fields. Always the village! At night, she would travel in her dreams to her village and at dawn, she would recount what she had witnessed there: the green brook was the same, it had not run dry. In the center of the village is the cross of Pilo [an old family in the village. HMM] buried under the ruins. She would lament the abandoned St. Tavit Church located on the outskirts of the village. She would talk about the Red Church, wherein an imaginary person named Avak would appear and tell a fairy tale about the maiden at the spring.

At night in her dreams she would return to her village life-reliving her youthful days - she would "come back" with many memories. On Easter morning, in her colorful dress, she would go to the celebration, where songs were sung. She was always the lead singer. She had a beautiful voice. Her singing was so sweet that when she sang a lullaby or a folk song, the snakes would come out to listen to her.

Mother, I remember the most intricate details of your stories; and even the little children have not forgotten them; they constantly repeat them. In only one night's travel, you would bring us so many intimate details...

And now, Mother, raise your head up and tell me what is there beyond this world? What do you have in the grave that could affect our lives here? Tell me, Mother, I am listening to you attentively. As in your dreams, would you proclaim "facts" or just total emptiness? Like an inquisitive mind, I would listen to your stories. Mother, what is a dream? Is it the sun that shines, or the shadows of tomorrow that for months you had prepared for –without telling us-? And now, in our desperate waiting, you keep us in mourning?

Mother, you never slept this late. You used to rise up with the first call of the rooster, but now even with thunder cracking in your ears, you don't move. You don't raise your head. You don't go to pray and you don't tell us your dreams, real or fictitious. You know something, Mother; I don't understand how you can tolerate all of this.

After sleeping for so long and so deeply, you would have had many stories to tell us. What can you tell us now about that awful night that you travelled and turned out the lights after you?

How was your first day of travel? Whom did you meet? Where did you rest?

When the earth and the stones started pelting your casket, what did you think? Did you think that a sinful maiden is being buried, or that people are seeking revenge against death by stoning your body?

You must have felt all that was happening.

I swear to you, Mother, I didn't throw one speck of sand! I would have given my right arm or been deprived of my eyesight had I participated in that terrible custom. The stones and earth being showered upon you were also falling on my head. As I walked to our home from the cemetery I, too, was a dead man.

My first step into the house was a terrible moment.

They would tell me, "Don't worry! Even angels have difficulty crossing from this side to the other side."

Tell me, Mother, what did you see on the other side of the gates? Did you find and did you kiss your loved ones, whose spirits you always wanted to see?

EPITAPHS, MORE PRECIOUS THAN PARCHMENTS

(Excerpt)

We are in the cemetery of the village. Father Hoosig walks me through the graveyard; I read the following epitaph, "Here lies Boghos Meloyan, who died at the age of ninety three after heartbreak; if you pass by here, pray for him and ask for God's judgment."

The priest says, "Boghos was the richest person in the village, very attentive to the welfare of the villagers. He had made sure that everyone had food on their table. He was the only person in the village that had the right to ride a horse, wear a red fez, red shoes, and use an expensive cloak.

He had invited the main government official, a Kurdish Bey, to his house.

Boghos's only son, Masroob, notices that the Bey makes an inappropriate pass at his bride. He couldn't take that; he flashes his sickle and runs at the Bey. The latter being faster takes out his dagger and stabs Masroob, who dies instantly.

Boghos took the case to the courts. It was dragged from one court to the next, from town to town, from one city to the next... to no avail... Who would care about this?

Soon after his son's death, his daughter-in-law went mad and threw herself in the well. Heartbroken, he passed away.

May God rest his soul and grant the right judgment he deserved.

THE WATCH OF MGHDESI AGOP

Our village was famous for two things: a church and the watch of Mghdesi Agop. I understood the importance of the church. It was where I used to go to pray every morning and evening; but the watch... It was hanging from Mghdesi Agop's neck down to his belly button with silver chains. -It was what a bride would display- that watch had an aura of mystery surrounding it.

All village folks, the farmers, anxious to take a peek at the watch, would find a logical reason to do that; during the irrigation of their field -Spring and Fall- Mghdesi Agop knew that

64

and was always ready to answer and show off his watch, fully realizing that was what the farmers really wanted to see.

One day I too, decided to venture on the same. Well, he was a rich man, so what! If he wouldn't want to talk to me, that was OK.

I found my motivation, but I was hesitating; although in my young mind I, too, had the right to take a peek at the watch.

That evening Mghdesi Agop was sitting by the well staring at his socks. I approached him cautiously; he saw me and waved at me to fetch him a cup of cold water. Wow, I was lucky! I got him a full jar of water!

- Good!

I was encouraged, so I asked, "What is the time, Sir?"

"Why do you want to know the time?" he asked.

"It is our turn to irrigate our field, but I don't know if it is time yet," I answered.

"It is not your time yet; as a matter of fact it is not even tomorrow."

I was stunned! My trick didn't work. Not to cause him any anger, I started to take off. He looked at me and said, "Hey, boy, it is the watch that you want to see, right? Why didn't you say so?"

With kind sweetness, he said, "Come; come take a look at it. But when the time comes, you have to bring me a jar of your fine wine."

I promised I would. And now the watch, which a moment ago seemed as far as the sun, was in my hands. What a beauty! What a miraculous thing! The watch had a little box with a key. I caressed the crystal, watched the movement of the hands; I held it to my ear... there was a sound coming from inside... Amazed and curious I was wondering, what was the tick-toking sound? Who is making that sound? Could it be that a bug is sitting inside?

FROM THE OTHER SIDE

(Excerpt)

The Characters:

SHAROOR AVAK- An old man -returning to earth after his death.

MAGAR- A villager.

Scene One

OLD MAN- The sun, the sun, the sun *(Silence)*.

MAGAR- Good morning, good morning.

OLD MAN- No, I am not mistaken; I have come to the right place. Everything is the same; the mountains are the same; the city is the same; sunrise and sunset are the same. But the change in the panoramic setting crushes my soul; what has happened in this beautiful valley?

MAGAR- Good morning, old man. Who are you? Where do you come from?

OLD MAN- *(Sits. Ponders)* There are pieces of broken ploughs and sickles under my feet. There are scattered bones on the banks of the river and everywhere. They remind me of slaughter houses. I saw fields similar to those described by Ezekiel.

MAGAR- Look at me, old man. Who are you? What were you saying? What are you searching? Where do you come from? Don't you hear me?

OLD MAN- I come from the world of the dead, my son. I left this place a long time ago. This is just an encounter. I have come to ask a favor. I am coming from the last Station of your forefathers.

MAGAR- He must be a mad man; what is he saying?

OLD MAN- They gave me a filthy spot at the Station. It was an awful place; I couldn't bear staying there anymore.

MAGAR- Lord, have mercy!

66

OLD MAN- There were a lot of people like me, who had departed from this world. Their spirits make the Station so dark.

MAGAR- I would love to hear the details of your story.

OLD MAN- There was no sun during the day and no moon or stars at night. Once in a while, lightning flashed above our heads; trembling in fear, we would watch the event.

MAGAR- Is that similar to what we see here above the clouds?

OLD MAN- No, No! That was entirely different! It was a creepy event. When lightning burst in strokes of bright glare at far distances, those at the Station would say, "God, sitting in His glowing chariot, is visiting the righteous people to deliver them the good news of salvation."

MAGAR- *(Shivering)* I confess and believe; I confess and believe! Envy what you have witnessed, good old man.

OLD MAN- Don't say that, my son. There was a time, when on Saturday evenings, the departed would come to the roofs of their own homes and smell the burning incense in their homes; at that moment, there was a kind of consolation between the dead and the living. But now? You do know what I mean. Right?

MAGAR- *(Sighs thoughtfully)* Huh...

OLD MAN- When those and other beautiful traditions changed, the relationship between the departing dead and the living ones was lost. Can you imagine the hopelessness of the dead for whom Heaven is inaccessible? They are bound to remain in their graves. They cannot see their loved ones, either; this deprivation is the real death.

MAGAR- *(Attentive, hangs his head)* So right, so right! Father Minas, God bless his soul, used to say the same thing. But you didn't tell me, what did they call you, here on earth? How old were you?

OLD MAN- My son, they called me Sharoor Avak. You are really inquisitive. I lived here some 90-95 years. I wanted to live a little bit longer. You can't get bored of this sun and the sky, the chirping birds and the greenery surrounding you. Even if you are on the verge of death, you still want to live. Yes, I wanted to live a little bit longer, but the wick of my life had been consumed like the last breath of the spring.

MAGAR- Can you tell me more about the circumstances of your departure from here?

OLD MAN- Two strange spirits with dark faces and dog muzzles, with vulture's feathers covering their wings, ordered me to surrender immediately. I had to comply. I was like a bird, which was breathing its last breath.

MAGAR- Were there lamenters and mourners?

OLD MAN- Who would have lamented?

MAGAR- Relatives, friends.

OLD MAN- Most of my family members had left already before me. The rest hardly knew me. Yes, I heard a woman's voice.

MAGAR- A woman's voice? Are you sure?

OLD MAN- That woman had a piercing howl.

MAGAR- This is really interesting, father Sharoor.

OLD MAN- The voice of that lamenting woman was like a burning curse. Like a blazing-hot nail, it pierced my soul and went beyond my coffin and ended up as a scorching spot somewhere.

MAGAR- But you said you were at the Station?

OLD MAN- They allowed me to be at the Station, so I could obtain valid reason to nullify her curse. They also ordered me to get attestations from here, so I could have a luminous wreath over my head.

MAGAR- What happened?

68

OLD MAN- I waited for 20-25 years; no favorable attestations came from here. They didn't believe my confessions, either. They used to get frequent opposite sentiments from here.

MAGAR- Wasn't there anyone there that could...?

OLD MAN- I understand what you are saying. All of them at the Station used to yell, "Sharoor is a disgraced convicted man." What were you asking? Oh, yes, let me tell you: way before that, my father had vigorously condemned me for what I had done. Listen, my time is short and I am trembling. Please don't make me talk anymore.

MAGAR- How about that lamenting lady?

OLD MAN- Don't mention her! My pain is too deep. I am tired and sleepy.

MAGAR- Just two words, please.

OLD MAN- The neighbor's wife, names are not important, in her youth, she was infatuated by my nephew. My nephew loved her too. I sent my nephew to Adana where unfortunately he died. After that, I asked the girl's father to send his daughter to a distant village, get her married, and settle down. This would have ended everything. The father complied. The girl was sent away. But unfortunately things didn't go as planned.

MAGAR- How's that?

OLD MAN- The bitch came back after a year or two. Her husband had died. The rumor was that she had killed him. The father didn't accept his daughter; he abandoned her. Now the woman is begging in the streets and feeds her two orphans whatever remnants she finds. That widow, who in a rage insulted me, was that girl. Her curse is still ringing in my ear.

MAGAR- Is that all?

OLD MAN- Yes, that's all. That incident on earth was declared as the worst action I had committed. But my time is short; if I go back late, they may put me in a worse place than I am now.

KRIKOR ZOHRAB

1861 - 1915

"As a member of the Ottoman Parliament, I am going to demand explanations from you, Talaat Pasha."*

Zohrab

*Mehmet Talaat was the Minister of Interior of Turkey, (1913-1917), and the master executor of the Armenian Genocide.

KRIKOR ZOHRAB
1861 - 1915

BIOGRAPHY- Writer, scholar, lawyer, orator, political and national activist, Krikor Zohrab was born on June 26, 1861 in the *Beshiktash* district of Constantinople, Ottoman Turkey. He attended the following schools in Constantinople: the *Makroohiats* elementary school, *Tarkmanchats*, *Shahnazarian* and *Galatasaray* high school. He went on to obtain advanced degrees in both engineering and law.

In 1883 he began to practice law and also taught at the School of Law in Constantinople. He authored three books about the law, one in French and two in Turkish and published respectively in Paris and Constantinople. During the Hamidian massacres of 1895-1896, he defended many Armenians accused of political and nationalistic activities. In 1905 he was disbarred because he defended a Bulgarian revolutionary, who had been tortured by the mayor of *Ishtip*. He went to Europe and returned to Turkey after the adoption of the 1908 constitution.

Zohrab was very influential in the Armenian community. As early as 1882, at the age of 21, he criticized the policies of Patriarch Varzhabedian, the highest ranking church official, regarding reforms for the Armenian people in Ottoman Turkey. With the passage of time, this keen intellectual struggled against the reactionary mentality of the time; he fiercely debated those who were against democratization of society; he scolded those who were against improving the lives of the Armenians in the provinces. Zohrab became a major force in the reform movement of the time and was elected a delegate to the Armenian National Assembly of the Patriarchate. In contrast to his progressive policies, when it came to women he was a traditionalist. He had many disagreements with Srpoohi Dusap, a prominent contemporary female writer and pioneer for the rights of Armenian women.

Zohrab was elected a member of the Ottoman Parliament, where he proposed the modernization of the Turkish educational system and the rule of law. He helped shape laws regarding agriculture as well as advanced arts and sciences. He also dismissed the old tax system; eliminated favoritism in the hierarchy of inheritance and worked diligently to pressure the authorities to adopt a policy of equality for ethnic minorities.

One of his most courageous acts occurred in 1909 during the massacres of the Armenians in Adana. The Ottoman government, controlled by the Union and Progress Party (UPP), had accused the Armenians of treason in order to justify their massacres as "punishment." Zohrab argued against the government's accusation in the courts and proved the innocence of the Armenians.

In 1911, Zohrab sent a memorandum to the prime minister of Turkey, demanding a stop to the indiscriminate killings by the UPP.

He condemned the German government's actions and cooperation with Turkey and was in favor of Russia's adopted policies for the Armenians.

During the period from 1912-1914, Zohrab participated in meetings with the ambassadors of the European nations to Turkey regarding the Armenian Case. In 1913, under the pseudonym of Marcel Liar, he published a booklet titled "The Armenian Question Examined under New Evidence."

Zohrab married Clara Yazejian in 1888 and they had two sons, Levon and Aram, and two daughters, Hermine and Dolores.

On May 20, 1915, he was arrested in his residence because of the aforementioned activities in support of the Armenians;

he was imprisoned and exiled and, en route to *Dikranagerd* (Diyarbakir), was brutally killed.

His sons, Levon and Aram, fled to France. His wife Clara and the two daughters, Hermine and Dolores, escaped to Austria through Bulgaria and reunited with Levon and Aram in Paris, France. After Clara's death, Dolores moved to Rumania and in 1932 married the American businessman Henry Liebman. They immigrated to New York in 1934. After her husband's death, in 1987 in New York City, Dolores established the Clara Zohrab Philanthropic Fund, which is still operating today.

LITERARY ACCOMPLISHMENTS- Zohrab began his literary journey with the writing of poetry. Later in his career, he turned to prose, a genre in which he is considered the master of the short story. He is a realist. He said, "Literature should be based upon the people to serve the people."

In 1885, when Zohrab was 24 years old, he came to the public's attention with his *"Anhedatsads Seroont Muh"* (A Vanished Generation), which first appeared in the paper *Yergrakoond* (The Globe). However, the paper soon stopped the publication of the series, fearing it created problems because it was "daring, overly exposed and too radical for the times." Another paper, *Massis*, continued where it was left off and published it in its entirety. With this novel, Zohrab made his definitive entry into the Armenian literary world.

His literary contributions are in the following areas:

Novels- During his lifetime he published *Anhedatsats Seroont Muh* (A Vanished Generation), 1885.

Novellas- *"Khughjmudanki Tsayner"* (Voices of Conscience), 1909, *Loorr Tsaver* (Silent Pains), 1911, *"Gyankuh Inchbes Vor E"* (Life as it is), 1911.

Familiar Faces- People whom he considered to be significant in the literary world: Arpiyar Arpiyarian (the founder of the Realist Movement), Retteos Berberian (the founder of the Berberian school, from where many famous writers graduated); Yeghia Demirjibashian, a free-spirited poet, and many others.

Poems- He composed poetry in two styles: structured rhyming and free-form poetry.

Prose and Chronicles- A collection of travelogue-type articles, in which he describes in-depth colorful scenes, meditates about nature and the surroundings.

Post mortem publications: "Pages from a Voyager's Book," 1922, Izmir; "A Vanished Generation," 1924, Istanbul; "Familiar Faces and Names," 1932, Paris; "From Our Life," 1945, Cairo; A two volume set of collected works, 1962, Yerevan; "About Literature," 1973, Yerevan.

PENNAMES- Ardavazt, H., K.Z., Le'art Marcel, Zohrab Krikor.

LITERARY CHARACTERISTICS- Zohrab was a literary giant, especially in the field of prose. He is a realist and was the most talented writer of prose amongst his contemporaries. His writings have depth and form that reached the pinnacle of aesthetic expression. He approaches his novels with a keen analytical eye and penetrates deep into the psyche of his heroes, drawing out the most poignant moments of their lives.

Zohrab also focuses on the traits and habits of society, and is able to evoke the ills and painful interactions between different factions. His topics include vain habits and their influence on human behavior. He is a keen observer of the differences in the attitude of society toward the conflict of rich versus poor.

Zohrab is truly a master literary figure as evidenced by his works having been translated into twenty six languages.

THE BURDEN OF RESPONSIBILITY

A.

He would walk the streets all day long carrying a large briefcase. That sturdy briefcase was his inseparable friend. He would use it to carry home to his two children the daily necessity of meat, bread, and fruits. His two children would greet him at the door with much anticipation - he never failed them.

All of his earnings from hard labor were in that briefcase. It was like the Jar of Cana* that he tried to fill for thirty years, without much success. His main struggle in life was trying to simply secure a living, supplying a daily ration of bread. He had the dreadful notion that his briefcase would be perpetually empty. His happiness, sadness, and memories were in that case, too. Just like the continual change of the fate of its owner, the case had its good and bad days; it had a soul much like its owner. But, who was the real master of the two?

After thirty years of being imprisoned by the iron grip of bad luck, he finally realized that the briefcase was truly the master.

*Referring to the Gospel of John II: 6, 7.

B.

Hoosep Agha was now an aged man of moderate build and a beard. Over the years, his business had slowly deteriorated, as did his status, from a dominant merchant to an ordinary middle-man. He would go from shop to shop, door to door carrying catalogues of different types of lingerie with competitive prices.

Items and prices don't always go hand in hand. Hoosep Agha was trying, in vain, to act as a middle man. He was in the dual role of trying to convince the buyer that the item was really inexpensive -and the seller, that he was charging too much.

Both buyer and seller would doggedly disagree with him and Hoosep Agha would acquiesce in disappointment. The trading business, which he understood very well as a merchant, was now threatening to destroy him.

This would not have mattered, if only he were alone. But he had to contend with two daughters and their teenage whims. They were not young girls anymore. They had become teenagers with the attendant natural desires and expectations associated therewith.

The girls were his entire happiness. But now they seemed to be pressing him with their innocent smiles, which to Hoosep were like a reprimand to his paternal soul. He would come home feeling much like a guilty person, facing the souls of his daughters condemned to deprivation. However, he would fake a smile to conceal his utter incompetence and agonizing distress and anguish.

C.

The three of them lived in a small house in the highlands of Uskudar, Ijadiye district. Their monthly rent was two hundred *ghroosh*. The mother had passed away many years ago. A portrait of a young woman hanging on the wall is that of the mother. She had died from a pulmonary condition in the days when her husband's job was quite prosperous. Her pale appearance in the picture was evidence of her illness. However, her memory lived on and not a day passed without her being mentioned. At night, after the girls retired, the father would linger by the picture, not saying a word but expecting some sort of encouragement from the unblinking eyes, waiting for support from beyond the grave.

His moral strength is ebbing as is his wealth. He now feels that his inner courage is failing and is slowly diminishing. In the morning, he still carries his briefcase but with trembling hands and often returns home with it empty. In the morning he visits the ports. There the merchants treat him like a beggar and occasionally give him odd jobs. He tries to be civil and even has the courage to join in the conversation, but always siding with the speaker. He doesn't walk alongside them; he's always a step behind, holding his briefcase. When one of the merchants suffers a loss in his business, he gets angry and denounces the competitors, calling them cheaters and liars, and accusing them of not paying their part of the contract. On happy occasions, he flatters them and tells them stories with the hope that the following day he'll be rewarded with a job.

The merchants liked the old man, because he was not like the others. He didn't demand his pay on time and would accept lower offers.

D.

The merchants of Basma had worries about the sale of their merchandise. Their main customers were Persian buyers. They were concerned about the falling prices of their goods and the dwindling profits. They were seeking ways to lower expenses. Along with taxes and office expenses, there was the mediator's fee. Who needed a mediator? Couldn't the merchandise be purchased without outside involvement? There were other reasons as well affecting this decision. After all, the mediator is a mediator and not the owner of the merchandise. He couldn't possibly explain the price nor have the power to concede.

Hoosep Agha, with the briefcase in his hand, was walking a few steps behind the merchants and was trembling.

"Hoosep Agha," the merchants would say, "we are not talking about you; you are one of us."

He would breathe a sigh of relief, but the job offers were fewer and fewer. It was becoming a real struggle to make a daily living. His debts were piling up. His clothing was still neat and holding up. No one could suspect the severity of his financial decline.

He would still carry his briefcase, but now it was merely a useless swaying appendage. After all, he couldn't abandon it and admit his hopelessness. What would the world say, seeing him without his constant companion?

One day he approached the merchant, whose shadow he was, and asked to borrow two gold pieces. He was refused and was told that he had to pay back the five gold pieces which he had earlier borrowed. That evening, in desperation, he sold his little brass watch to partially fill his case.

E.

At home, he appeared happy and joyful. His daughters would ask about the details of his job. They had their own suspicions.

"How is work?" the older daughter would ask.

The younger would follow with, "Don't be that late."

The father would laugh, no, work was not good. But with the help of God, things would change.

"Come home early tomorrow night and let's go out."

The poor father would promise to come home early to take the orphans out. But the poor souls were spending their youthful years in poverty. Just imagine their "going out" as a trip in a tunnel, where stone walls prevent light from shining at the end.

In the morning, early in the morning, pressing the empty briefcase under his arm, he would take the steamship to Constantinople. The briefcase -his eternal enemy and eternal insatiable object- had not been satisfied for some thirty years. He would squeeze the briefcase so hard, as if to choke it. He really wanted to destroy this empty "stomach".

There were no jobs in Constantinople. The money left over from the sale of his watch was to disappear in paying for transportation. That moment was fast approaching with irresistible speed. He would have used his last thirty *para*, to go from Koozkoonjook to Constantinople; thirty *para* would disappear in his pursuit of hope. It cost money to chase after hope.

That was the problem that kept popping up in his mind and confronting him. It appeared in huge letters in the air, and followed him wherever he went.

F.

How can a man stand motionless who faces the need to feed his family, but does not have the fare to commute to look for work?

Hoosep Agha was pondering these thoughts and was trying to find answers. Clasping his empty briefcase, he had thought of himself in his home with his two beautiful daughters. For just a moment, he would forget the daily need for food and lose himself in his thoughts. For just a moment, he would imagine himself a rich man giving his daughters new dresses, hats, and even more than they wished for. He would give them anything and everything just to see them abound in happiness; a happiness that seems so easy and yet so difficult!

The leather briefcase under his arm was shivering and awakened him from his dream, bringing him back to reality: the reality of a hungry man.

Then, small but frightening changes in behavior took place. He would take pieces of furniture to the market under the pretext of having them fixed; instead he would sell them in new shops inexpensively. He would try to borrow money from his old friends and would wait hours in order to obtain a steamship ticket. All in a futile attempt to fill, or partially fill, the demanding briefcase that he carried with him.

G.

One morning, his eldest daughter gave him the briefcase saying, "Papa, yesterday you forgot to get the meat, don't forget to get it today. Also bring some fruit and cheese."

She would go on with her endless list of desires, just as her father was running out the door.

As he was walking downhill, the briefcase was swinging and making the gurgling and sobbing sounds of an empty stomach.

Out of fear of losing them, he had carefully pocketed three metal coin pieces, which were to serve as his pass to Constantinople. But, how was he to come back that night? He regretted, really regretted living in Uskudar, which was too far to reach by walking. Being good-hearted or having the greatest courage in the world was just not enough to go home empty-handed.

He avoided sitting next to his friends in the steamship. He sat far away from them, at the end, where there were no comfortable seats and next to lice-infested travelers.

He set the briefcase next to him and carefully straightened the folds. The grinding ruff-ruff sound of the steamship's wheels got his attention. As they turned, they would hesitate for a second, restart again and create a unique piece of music: ruff, ruff, ruff, ruff…. ruff. He enjoyed listening to that song. For a few moments, there was nothing else in his mind or in his soul. Who was he? What was he looking for on this steamship? Where was he going? He didn't know. He really didn't know.

In Constantinople, he faced the angry and cruel behavior of the merchants with whom he had dealt with in the past. He was confused and at a loss for words. "Be brave! Tell these rigid men that you have promised to take food to your children tonight." No, he could not.

82

He walked through the market without speaking to anyone. He stood for about fifteen minutes in front of the goldsmith's displays admiring the diamond bracelets, which he had been unable to give to his daughters. He suddenly realized his daughters were waiting for him. He asked for the time of day. It was already night. He started to run. He was late. It wasn't time to be lost in thoughts. Food was needed, and he would ask for it from the first acquaintance that he saw. Strange as it may seem, he, who knew so many people, didn't come across any of his friends. He knew the person walking on the opposite side of the street; he, who used to be his competitor. But they had ceased to greet each other because of the decline of his economic status. There was this other person, who recently had refused to lend him money and now was walking by him at a fast pace, avoiding his presence. Only an old man greeted him; and he was in an even more pathetic state.

Hoosep Agha arrived at the bridge but would not be able to cross it. He didn't have the ten *para* for the fare. He asked himself, "why?" and found the reason; he had forgotten his briefcase somewhere. He ran back... to do what?

H.

He was lying on his back, floating on the surface of the water and swaying with the waves. He was heavy set, with large, unblinking eyes looking up and admiring the sky. There the moon was at half-cycle shining like a large coin.

And tied to his neck and floating along was a black leather briefcase. The briefcase would pull the head down, but once in a while, it would free itself from the weight of the briefcase.

With the background of the shining surface of the sea, the body, with the briefcase tied to its neck, looked like a ship that had left a small boat behind. From a distance, the two of them, tied together in the water, were inseparable, just as they had been in life. There was no fear of emptying the briefcase anymore, for now it was filled with rocks. It was like a bloated full stomach. The briefcase didn't have to be squeezed and be wedged underarm. With its unreasonable obstinacy and hopeless emptiness, it represented the burden of responsibility. Its proper place was around the neck of the man, and that's where it was now.

For thirty years, it had been like a lost soul; now joyous and happy that it has found its rightful place. The briefcase, with its coarse texture, now caresses and strokes the man's face.

TEFFARIG

(An oily perfume)

A.

She came to our house from Arslanbeg, a village lost in the mountains surrounding Izmit. She wore the villagers' *shalvar* (baggy pants) and every strand of her hair was neatly tucked under her kerchief. She showed a crude sense of authority which resulted in an objectionable disposition.

Beneath her head-to-toe black attire, she had a pale sickly white face, like that of cold, pure, shining snow.

She forsook worldly ornaments, in homage to the memory of her late husband. This young woman was finding solace and fulfillment in her behavior. By doing so, she fancied a relationship with an imaginary being in the "world beyond," thinking that she would be attractive and submissive to his envious traits. Her self-imposed intelligence was a statement of attraction for her "departed" late husband. "I wanted to be beautiful for you only, not anyone else."

At home, she was fully occupied in the duties of a maid. She was not talkative, and when necessary, would only speak in one-syllable words.

She never smiled or laughed. At night, after dinner, she would immediately retire alone into her tiny room, which was like the austere quarters of a hermit. She would sit there for hours weaving socks for the child she had left in the village.

B.

She worked all day long, carefully and diligently sweeping, wiping, and cleaning. In her baggy pants, she would move nimbly into every corner of the house, removing lint from the couches and dust from the mirrors.

In spite of her efforts, she was unable to put my room in order. Ten times a day, she would organize my room and ten times a day I would mess it up again. I would throw my clothes and my underwear all over. My books were scattered on the couch and on the floor. A hundred times she would neatly put them back, and an hour later I would make a mess again. There seemed to be a competition between her inexhaustible orderliness and my unruliness. Yet, she would not complain; that is, if I did not consider her quiet persistence as a sign of resentment against my behavior. No, she wouldn't complain, instead she would stubbornly tolerate my bad behavior to the extent of causing me shame, and with her boundless forgiving attitude, she would conceal my cruel prodigal behavior.

I felt that it was not appropriate to trifle with this young maid. I respected her quiet work habits and the sincerity of her grief; I would speak like a brother with sweet tenderness. Whenever I wanted something, I would say, "*Koozoom* (my girl), Mariam."

C.

We called her Mariam. My mother would not agree to accept any other name for our maids. Her real name was Ashkhen. But, as soon as she began to work in a stranger's house, she was subjected to this "double christening," which allowed her to pretend she was disowning her past.

Even her name was not respected. Strangers were thoughtlessly banishing her from her self. New manners of speech and new clothing were being offered to her, only allowing her to keep her shoes.

She would not tolerate this humiliation. Her name, although not appreciated by the inhabitants of Constantinople, was most favored by the boys of her native village. Her motions, her dress, and even her baggy pants had made her the most graceful lady in her village. And now, one-by-one she was to discard all conquests and admit how ridiculous they were.

Sometimes I would call her Ashkhen and, leaving all her chores behind, she would run to me. She was pleased to find me observant of her nature. She was proud that a man from Constantinople found her name most pleasant.

We would talk to each other. I would ask about the son she left behind in Arslanbeg.

She would reply softly unravelling the secrets in her heart. Her heart had been wounded; but she didn't want to be consoled, and perhaps her hurt had become a habit. A habit which was difficult to abandon, like that of a smoker who could not quit smoking.

D.

Now she was caring for my room, the windows of which looked out upon a rosebush, which periodically blossomed circlets of red and white flowers.

After completing her duties during the day in my absence, she would enter my room and continue to weave socks for her son, surrounded by the scent of the rosebush.

As an obedient maid, she would fondly council me about the papers scattered on the floor, she would say, "Isn't it a pity that you have wasted your eyesight writing these notes?"

Only eyesight? If only she knew how I poured my heart into these pages. If only she knew that the innocence of teenage years and youthful dreams had been poured into them. After that, there is left only a stoic boy, who, like melted metal, had lost all qualities of prior existence and now, had become nothing but an ordinary, vague homogenous being. If only she knew...

The maid didn't know anything about this. When I returned at night and everyone was asleep, I bent over the blank, pure white paper and blackened it with meaningless writing – just like my heart was being decorated by black scribbles.

In the morning, pitying me, she would tiptoe into my room, avoiding making any nose, pretending it was still night so that I might sleep a little bit longer.

Upon awakening, with my eyes swollen, her reprimanding look would mellow and would hasten me to the kitchen to prepare my breakfast to "cure" my lack of sleep.

E.

Sometimes with my mother's help, she would try to put me on a healthy course.

"Madam, tell him not stay out too late at night."

I would joke, "And you weave socks."

"The knitting is for my son; I am poor."

Her voice would suddenly change. Her usual sadness would come forth again as she thought about her son back in Arslanbeg. Every struggle from her past: her mourning, her difficulties, her bitterness would pass in front of her eyes like a panoramic view. They would lineup like rosary beads. Her marriage had lasted less than two years. Their money had been spent on her husband's illness. Her son had been left behind in the village and now she was being forced into the houses of strangers. All of this was evident and was apparent on her delicate face -an entire canvas of sorrow and agonizing pain. Then the narrative would stop.

It was my turn to speak.

"Ashkhen, take off the baggy pants." I said.

She was ashamed. The dresses worn in the city, with their form-fitting features, in her eyes, were a shameless thing.

She would say, "I am ashamed."

I felt that her resistance to change was lessening. Her view of appearing displeasing didn't last more than weeks. Her major concern, "I am ashamed," was fading, too; it was vanishing.

F.

The dress really did fit her nicely and radically changed her. First, she lost her provincial notions along with the possible effects of the weather. It appeared to her that the waist was too tight and the skirt too loose. The first four days she couldn't move. She was careful not to be ridiculed when walking.

The upper portion of the dress accentuated the particulars of her breasts, and gave her the impression that she was being attentively observed for that.

All of us were amazed at the blossoming of her beauty. Upon hearing compliments, she would blush and turn her head modestly toward her shoulder.

She gradually became more stylish. This was a new awakening for her. She knew she could be as beautiful as the ladies in Constantinople; she was coquette and could flirt with the villager's simplistic way. During the day, she was always neat and well groomed. Her veil, now pushed back, would barely stay on her head. It always threatened to fall onto her shoulders, thus exposing the thick waves of her hair. Part of her hair fell onto her forehead and down to her eyes. Part of it flowed down to her neck, where her white skin peeked through the strands.

She used an unusual perfume much different from those familiar to us. It was barely noticeable and seemed to be the result of her body's natural emollients. It had a very mystical and passionate quality.

G.

All of that pretentious show was for me, I surmised. The old wound seemed to have been healed in her soul, which was really attached to me.

Her love was tremulous and shy. It was completely unselfish and quiet, a love that doesn't mention the sacrifices made for you, so as not to point to your ungrateful indifference. No, this was a secret and mysterious feeling that is ashamed of its enormity. It would be hidden like an earthquake that resembles a volcano without its thunderous and fiery roar.

She didn't ask anything in return for her love, not even my love. All she wanted was permission to forever surround me

89

with her affection; to watch over me, so that I wouldn't become ill; to swaddle and protect me so that I would witness neither pain nor sorrow.

This lasted for a month. She would sit on the floor next to me and allow her hair to cover my knees. She would take pleasure from my caressing her hair, much like a petted kitten.

I became bored with this charming behavior. I was twenty years old and didn't know the value of sincere love. The selfless nature of this maid became an unbearable bond. To escape from her caring affection was nearly impossible. It was like being hospitalized and trying in vain to escape.

She didn't understand my feelings. In her naiveté, she thought she hadn't done anything wrong and therefore there was no reason to reject her. She didn't know that it was the enormity of her love that was crushing me. It was like a summer day with stifling heat.

She did not realize that we pretended with fake caresses and enticements to make love wildly. She didn't understand that her innocent sacrifices were really boring. She felt that I was parting from her and tried, for the last time, not to sever our warm relationship.

When she entered my room, I noted that she had accentuated and exaggerated her lovely appearance in order to impress me. She was always a beautiful woman: tall, fair skin, with a quivering, graceful walk. There was sadness in her wide, puppy-like eyes. Right then and there, a scent of *Teffarig* (a unique aromatic perfume) filled the room; an aroma dense enough to be stifling.

I don't know how, but that suffocating perfume made me despise this woman. Did I need an excuse to end my relationship with her? Or was my reaction triggered by the tales associated with this ancient, oily perfume? I don't know.

Teffarig? Where did she find this perfume? Before she could open her mouth, from the end of the room I screamed in a savage tone, "What is that scent? Go and wash it off immediately!"

She didn't answer. She stood still at the door, without moving a step. She looked at me in amazement and not understanding my outburst for a simple fault. She was barely able to balance herself, much like the wounded soldier a moment before falling down.

H.

What else would you like me to tell you? Do you really want to hear the last words of this innocent love affair?

She became sick and lay in her bed for a week. She was suffering from pneumonia and I was the cause of it.

Standing in the kitchen that night and responding to my command, she had washed herself in order to get rid of the perfume. Our doctor friend was much surprised at the strange habits of villagers.

"Is this woman mad? Who would bathe in the kitchen?" the doctor asked.

I didn't answer. The doctor was surprised and persisted in trying to get an answer from me.

"What do you say? Is she mad?" I asked.

But I was fearful of her impending demise and was concerned about her recovery.

"She will live, right, Doctor?"

I was tormented for eight days. Then slowly she began to recover. Her recovery was slow, much like the progression of a new illness.

Whenever I visited her and asked about her health, she would show her affection. She would not look at me with reprimand. It seemed she appeared more at ease now. She would show new signs of self-sacrifice, which would make me more obligated. She wanted to feel like a creditor by her immense self-sacrifice. A creditor that is willing to readily forgive all her borrowers by merely hearing a sweet word.

She never again spoke about that incident, which she seemed to forget. But her health did not improve and she never regained her former strength. She was getting weaker and weaker and was wasting away. The doctor would shake his head, -an ominous sign- a foreboding sign- indeed- a prediction of an imminent sad outcome, known well in advance. This was the inevitable last stage of pneumonia that began with fever accompanied by mild sweating.

I.

She died in her village, where we had sent her on the recommendation of the doctor. She died leaving me with tremendous feelings of guilt, which after ten years, my pen is recording here. And, contrary to my desire, it records my ungrateful attitude towards the memory of a selfless and unique love.

I ponder that life is full of such disasters. Like pain that results from misunderstanding one other and becomes an incurable disease.

There is endless fondness scattered here and there, which is believed to be useless, which should have strengthened love and made it everlasting.

Feelings are being diverted from their main goals. An abundance of disjointed self-sacrifices, which for not being reciprocated, are lost and leave behind a trace of memories full of misery.

ALWAYS HIGHER

Excerpt

Against the vast velvety green landscape of Central Europe, south of Salzburg, on the horizon, appears a gigantic mute mass of rock, piercing its snow-covered peaks in the clear sky, at times being caressed by cottony clouds.

They are the mountain range of the Alps.

This place is not for those who love plains. It is a strange land; there is no place to walk, no place to rest, only to climb. One has either to climb or fall. This is our century's motto and fate: higher, always higher to the supreme effort, a beyond where death awaits us. This is the life of the Twentieth Century: next to large joys, there are large disappointments; next to large selfishness, there is large sacrifice; and next to large sins, there are large deliverances. This century is the century of heroism; it will not have an equal to its death-defying attitude. This death is not the death displayed in wars, where people kill their own kind, but it is to benefit mankind.

There is a breathtaking view from up here; one couldn't differentiate anything from down below. I guess that's how to look at people, with a clear view from above, so that we can embrace everything; not with a narrow, jealous attitude, where smallness is seen and greatness and beauty are lost forever.

SMPAD PYOORAD

(Smpad Der Ghazariants)

1862 – 1915

"We are longing for the Light.
The gates of hope will be opened by Light."

Pyoorad

SMPAD PYOORAD (Smpad Der Ghazariants)
1862 – 1915

BIOGRAPHY- Born in Zeytoon, he attended the *Zharankavorats* (Seminary) in Jerusalem from 1871-1880. From 1880-1882 he was the principal and teacher in a school in Marash. In 1882 he taught at the *Miyatsyal* (United) School in Zeytoon. In 1885 he established a school in Sis, the capital city of the Armenian medieval kingdom of Cilicia. The same year in Constantinople he married an educator from the Kalfayan Orphanage. From 1885-1887 he was the principal of Gumuljine and Zeytoon schools successively and in 1887–1890 he was in Samsun where he established a school. As a political activist and field worker he visited the provinces, where he was accused as a propagandist and was imprisoned in Marash for five years. He was transferred along with his wife to the prisons in Aleppo. After his release be went back to Constantinople and taught at the Aramian School in Constantinople's district of Kadi Koy. In 1896, during the Hamidian massacres, he escaped to Egypt, where he devoted himself to educational and literary endeavors. In Cairo, he established a school that lasted for four years. He published the *Pyoonig* (Phoenix) and *Nor Or* (New Day) newspapers. From 1904-1906 he became the principal of the Armenian School in Alexandria. In 1907 he went to Rumania, and then returned to Egypt. In 1909, after the announcement of the New Constitution of Turkey, he went back to Constantinople and became involved in education and journalism. For a short while, he published the *Pyoonig* (Phoenix) and *Nor Or* (New Day) newspapers again. He was elected as a delegate to the Armenian National Assembly from Marash. He was arrested in April 1915 and sent to the prison of Ayash.

LITERARY ACCOMPLISHMENTS-

Novels- *Pande Pand* (From Prison to Prison), *Zeytooni Vrezhuh* (The Revenge of Zeytoon), *Tebi Yelduz* (To Yelduz), *Innsoon Vets* (Ninety Six), *Zeytooni Vartabeduh* (The Bishop of Zeytoon), *Vortesban Dsnokhkuh* (The Filicide Parents), *Sasoonen Yedk* (After Sassoon), *Verchin Pertuh* (The Last Fortress), *Demir Moushloo, Vegharavor Herosuh* (the Hero With a Cloak), *Tiyagaboodneruh* (The Pillagers), *Azadootyan Hamar* (For Freedom), *Aryooni Jampoon Vra* (On the Bloody Road), *Avedaran Zeytoontseren* (The Bible in Zeytoon Dialect), *Poorkeren* (From the Pyramids).

Play- *Avarayri Ardsivuh* (The Eagle of Avarayr).

History- B*admootyoon Hayots, Vol. I* (Armenian History), Vol. I, *Aryooni Tsor* (The Valley of Blood) and *Yelduzeh Sassoon* (From Yelduz to Sassoon, the history of Zeytoon in six volumes).

PENNAMES- *Abdag* (Slap), Berj, Smpad, Hayg-Levon, *Khaytots* (The Stinger), *Lerrntsi (*The Mountaineer), *Lerrnorti* (Son of the Mountain), *Mdrag* (The Whip), Pyoorad, Smpad Pyoorad, Pyoordaghyants Smpad, Tat, and S. P.

LITERARY CHARACTERISTICS- He has made the largest literary contribution to the historical development and struggle of the Armenian people. His wrote historic novels about the Cilician era. He dealt with nationalistic sympathies; he incited and awakened nationalism. He treated his topics with mysticism. As a knowledgeable historian, he interjected historical facts into his novels. His poetry is nationalistic; it is a representation of that era. He was the first to revive the famous battle of Avarayr in a play. He attempted to highlight the importance of history to the nineteenth century. The backbone of his writings is his concern to awaken the Armenian nation to realize its past, evaluate its present, and have a bright expectation for the future.

TRANSLATED WORKS

LETTERS

Here are a few of the letters that Smpad Pyoorad sent from Ayash prison.

28 April 1915.

Don't worry about me; I am well and alive. I am not alone. There are 84 of us. We'll be freed soon by God's help.

16 May 1915

Mr. Theodore Mendsigian is still here; although Ali Akbar Khan had ordered his release. Eight of us are citizens of Persia. We have submitted a petition to be released; we are still waiting to hear a response. We have wired the Patriarchate; we have not heard anything yet. Send us a Bible to alleviate our anguish.

26 May 1915

I have high hopes; justice will prevail. This is just a storm that will pass. Don't worry!

30 May 1915

Last week Agnoony, Khazhag, R. Zartarian, Jangyoolian, Daghavarian, and Sarkis Minassian were ordered by Ankara to be transferred; we don't know their whereabouts. It is ironic that after being subjected to so many sacrifices during the tyrannical regime and having reached the hopeful state of constitutional freedom, we are again subjected to destitution. Was this going to be the destiny of those who had already suffered by devoting their lives to the Fatherland? If Talaat realized the destitution I have endured with my family, he would really end this ordeal, which really diminishes his magnanimity. Which police official would not feel sorry for your state, my poor wife? You, who under the tyrannical regime suffered and lost your eyesight, I am sure there'll come a day – and that day is very close- when Justice will prevail. Alas that will be useless, for our suffering will stay with us.

6 June 1915

When you visit the Patriarch at the Patriarchate, please extend my respect to him and mention that having secured the release of Mr. Khojasarian is not enough; he should attempt to have others released. Please read these lines to him."

THE EAGLE OF AVARAYR
OR VARTANANK

A Tragedy

(A Play in five Acts and four Scenes)

(Excerpt)

[Note: This soliloquy is from Pyoorad's famous play, first presented on Vartanants' Day in 1910 in Cairo, Egypt by the famous Fasoolyajian-Benlian theater company.

This scene was chosen because of Pyoorad's patriotic sentiments expressed by a female character at a time when Armenians had just witnessed the massacres of Armenians in Adana in 1909 by Sultan Hamid.

The historical event: In 450 AD, Persia tried to convert Armenians from Christianity to Zoroastrianism. Armenians refused to be converted. Persia tried to enforce the conversion; the Armenians resisted, thus leading to the battle of Avarayr in 451 AD.

Shooshanig is the daughter of Vartan Mamigonian, the General and commander-in-chief of the Armenian army.]

Act Four, Scene One

SHOOSHANIG- *(Alone and upset, with her hair disheveled, is sitting in a corner of her room.)* There is no doubt, the battle is imminent. My father, the Commander in Chief, and his first body-guard, my Vrooyr [her fiancé. HMM], will be in the battle; and I will moan and lament with my inconsolable mother. How bitter it is to be a girl and the daughter of the commander in chief; to be enthusiastic about the battle yet to be imprisoned and kept far away from the battlefield! *(Stands up and determined)* No, no, I'll turn things around, I will wipe off the shame of centuries; I'll be the first to demonstrate heroism in our race. What! Persia desecrates our churches, invades our fatherland, and I, of the Mamigonian clan, the legitimate daughter of Vartan Mamigonian, the fiancé of my brave Vrooyr, be condemned not to join in the procession and brave regiments? Is this possible? *(Takes a wide step and ponders aloud)* Shooshanig is engulfed by the fever of the battle. Personal love does not mean anything to her, now that she is wrapped-up by the love of her Fatherland. But, isn't love of battle a fire of life? When that is inflamed inside a person, it devours life? But Shooshanig will pursue a more sublime battle at this moment, that of: Armenia against Persia; Fatherland against enemy; Freedom against subjugation, which undoubtedly will be crowned by our victory. After all, isn't the general and the commander-in-chief my father? And my soul and my life is his first body guard? And I, as an Armenian, why shouldn't I be a hero, who would get involved in the battle and participate and shatter the enemy's filthy lines... *(Points to herself)* Yes, I am a courageous person, I am! A male lion is a lion; what is a female lion? Yes, I'll join my Armenian heroes. I'll fight side-by-side with my Vrooyr; I wouldn't leave him for a moment... I'll inspire the army by my presence...

THE POET

Look! He is going; don't ask where he is headed.
Ignoring the commotions surrounding him, he is going.
He punctuates his every step with dark dots.
  He is a poet... do you know that?
        He hates the crowds; reads silence instead.
        His reach is larger than the universe
        But the world thinks he is insane
        After all he is a poet...
He doesn't have a home; he ridicules fate.
He questions rays, scents, shadows, and waves
And waits anxiously for replies.
  He is a poet... do you know that?
        People insult him; he pities them in return,
        He sings the fate of the deprived with anguish,
        He laments with widowers the lives of their orphans
        He is a poet... do you know that?
He is above vice and walks only by sidling
He is the embodiment of the sufferings of his nation,
He has sworn to sacrifice his life and wealth
To his nation's misery.
  Respect him! He is the nation's poet.
        He is a prophet with thundering advice,
        Born in this century, but will live for centuries to come,
        He is the noble blind man incessantly looking up.
            He is a poet... do you know that?
The poet... yes, he travels and travels,
His thorny path leads him to hospitals
Or the gallows... and to the gates of graves.
  He is a poet... do you know that?

MY SONG OF EXILE

(Excerpts)

Oh, autumn breeze, blow!
My soul needs nourishment.
Sprinkle your dewdrops
On my heart, where a fire is ablaze
And won't smother.
I fell from the splendor of your spring
Onto this foreign land,
A foreign sky under which
No one can live.
I am possessed by you, my Country,
My precious gift.

***

Life is over there, beyond the sea,
Where the Fatherland is separated by
Canyons and mountains with dark slopes.

Fatherland...
A fireplace in the corner
A garden, a vineyard and a brook.

Zeytoon,
A wounded but undefeated lion,
With open arms
Stares at the path of return
Of its exiled ill-fated son.

Oh, who will bring me?
Tell me who will bring me the autumn of my village
Which spreads gently on the hills, in the valleys,

In the fields and the woods?
There, my Self feels cordial, friendly
And harmonious.
The autumn of my village that runs fiercely,
To finally rest in the brook.

I want to see the line of trees
On the banks of the brook,
And sleep there quietly.
Take me, oh, breeze of autumn,
Take me there,
To my Shoughri*
To Bagh-Aghpyoor**
To the peak of old Berzinga***
The proud mountain of Zeytoon****.

Tell me Autumn,
Who will grant me my days past?

*His hometown.
** "Cold Spring"- a spring in his hometown.
*** A mountain in his hometown.
**** A region in Cilicia.

OUR SHARE

(Excerpt)

Born free and happy in a loving family,
With mom and dad, sisters and brothers,
Then take up a cane, become a "bantookht"
Working all day long and dark nights too.
Sick and captive, abandoned and lonely,
Begging pity from pitiless folk.
Is this ordinary pain, almighty God?
But this is the pain granted by You to all those
Called Armenians.

Leaving a homeland behind, abandoning homes and
Churches and handing them over to the Kurds;
Avoiding the dagger of persecution,
Running afar just to survive.
Witnessing the gush of blood
Of dads, moms, women and children and siblings too;
Sacrificing honor and what they own.
Is this an ordinary pain, almighty God?

But this is the pain granted by You to all those
Called Armenians.

No! Strangers cannot heal our wounds.
No! The hope I have I'll never lose.
I know sooner or later, my captive nation
Will free itself; shatter the chains of slavery,
And yell out loud, "Enough, dear God.
You only granted pain to those
Who are called Armenians."

YEROOKHAN
(Yervant Srmakeshkhanlian)
1870 - 1915

"Nature's sounds are like a sweet lullaby, the only sweet voice, where there is no deception."

Yerookhan

YEROOKHAN (Yervant Srmakeshkhanlian)
1870 -1915

BIOGRAPHY- Yerookhan was born in July 1870 in Khas-kyoogh, a district of Constantinople. He attended the local Nersessian School, a dilapidated building with an underground classroom. According to his autobiography, he describes himself as a lazy student, who hated arithmetic. In 1886 his father wanted to register him in the medical school, but a neighbor convinced him to send his son to the newly opened *Getronagan* (Central) School. Here, too, Yervant remained scholastically poorly motivated. He described not being interested in anything. He became ill and missed final examinaitons. After recovering from his illness, he asked to take the examinations but the faculty refused and was asked to leave High School. He found a job with a merchant but was soon terminated. Yervant, realizing his shortcomings, he reevaluated himself and began a program of self-education. He read every major literary work and also learned French. His father reprimanded him for not working. Eventually he found a job as a translator at the newspaper *Arevelk* (the East). After a year of working at the paper, he wrote his first story, *Babooguh* (The Grandpa). The major literary figures of the time, Zohrab, Arpiyarian, and Hrand Asadoor, liked the story and recognized a writing talent in him. From then on, he wrote for *Arevelk, Masis,* and other newspapers.

During the Hamidian massacres of 1896, he escaped to Bulgaria. There he founded the newspapers *Sharzhoom* (Action) and *Shavigh* (Pathway). He also contributed to the paper *Puzantion* (Byzantium).

In 1904 he went to Eygpt, where he published the periodical *Siswan*. He taught in the Armenian schools of Cairo and

Alexandria, married one of his students, and stayed in Eygpt until 1908. Upon the announcement of the new Ottoman constitution, he returned to Constantinople and taught the Armenian language at *Getronagan* (The Central) High School, the same school that had expelled him. In 1913 he moved to Kharpert (Harput) as the schoolmaster of the high school. In a few years, he elevated the school's standard to college-level.

He was elected a delegate to the Armenian National Assembly.

In 1915 he was arrested and imprisoned with educators from *Yeprad* (Euphrates) College. After much humiliation and brutal treatment, with hands bound, they were paraded in the streets and were finally killed in the valley of Masdar Mountain. His wife and two children died in the forced death marches to the desert of Der El Zor.

LITERARY ACCOMPLISHMENTS-

Novels- *Gyankin Mech* (Within Life), 1911, *Merzhvads Deruh* (the Rejected Master), *Amirayin Aghchiguh* (Amira's Daughter), *Harazad Vortin* (The Legitimate Son), 1913.

Translations- "Jack" by A. Dode', 1896, "The Family" by H. Maloy, 1894, "The Wolves of Paris" by J. Le Monay, 1893, "The Pale Girl" by J. Mary, 1894, and "The Eastern Problem and the Armenian Question" by Ed. Drau.

He wrote numerous articles about Armenian issues in various Armenian papers.

PENNAMES: *Ashoogh* (Troubadour), *Kaghtagan* (Immigrant), Shavarsh, Shavarsh Y., *Sofiapnag* (Resident of Sofia), *Y. Kaghtagan* (Y. Immigrant), Y.C., U.S, Yervant, Yerookhan.

LITERARY CHARACTERISTICS- Yerookhan is a representative of the Realist movement in Armenian Literature.

110

He writes in a lively manner about humble men, mostly fishermen. He writes about their daily worries and concerns, mostly about their pain and sorrow. He sincerely believes that those who have earned their daily bread with hard work have high moral values. They are humble men living in damp and deteriorating houses.

Yerookhan delves into the world of the struggling common man: the fishermen, porters, coachmen, firemen, and water carriers. He portrays them as honorable individuals, vital to their community, full of vigor and concern for their fellow human beings.

TRANSLATED WORKS

THE AMIRA'S DAUGHTER

A note about the novel. The story line: Sophie, the beautiful daughter of a laundry-lady, is employed in the house of an *Amira* (literally, "prince," a title given to a class of wealthy families in Ottoman Turkey). His son, Arshag, is a physician. The employment of poor girls in that society was just a ploy, an excuse for the bosses to exploit women for sexual fulfillments. Enter Hampig, the son of a laborer, who has himself acquired a level of education. He falls in love with Sophie. She, however wavers between Hampig's sincere love and the luxurious environment she lives in. In the end, she realizes the bleak future of living as the concubine of the rich doctor versus the sincere sentiments of Hampig, and she decides to marry Hampig.

The following excerpt is the last scene of the novel, in which Hampig has come to take Sophie away.

111

It was a crisp sunny day. Nature had joined Hampig in his happiness.

In this state of happiness, Hampig was considering his past sufferings. Now, everything in the past seemed so unimportant. Everything had turned out for the best. What a triumph this was over the rich son of the Amira and a revenge against the man who had caused him so much misery.

He was on his way to see Sophie. Every once in a while, without fully realizing it, he would think back to his teen-age years and reminisce about the minute details of the events of his odyssey.

Pictures of his mother and father would appear in his mind. Where were they now? Misery had overcome them and caused his mother's death. Hampig was very anxious to see them now. He wanted to see their tired faces finally brighten with smiles as they witnessed their son's happiness.

The last scene of his life's drama was coming to an end- his vagabond existence of wandering in the mountains, the valleys, and shores; his gulping down the leftovers from the plates of disorderly fishermen and sleeping neck-to-neck with dogs under benches in cafes. He had been swallowed up in that lifestyle and strangely enough, he had enjoyed it...

All of a sudden, a hand had been extended to him... the same hand that had cast him into the abyss of misery. Hampig was furiously blaming himself for doubting the sincerity of Sophie's love.

"Let us wait," the girl had said. It is not yet the right time.

And now, 'the blessed right time' had arrived.

Finally, the girl was going to be his, his alone. And he would love her zealously, as no one had ever loved her before.

He would earnestly try to live up to every promise he had made in his letters to her. He would amaze and surprise her with all the unassailable details. "Doctor, doctor... poor soul... let me see how you would snatch Sophie from me now...?"

He arrived at Pera (a district near Constantinople) and then crossed to Constantinople. He was carrying many packages; he was eager and sweaty, feverishly expecting to return home.

He had purchased a few charms to give Sophie as the first surprise. Night had started to fall. Hampig took the packages to the mansion and placed them in a safe place so that, if at all possible, he might give them that same night.

He went up to Sophie's room to see if she was ready to leave.

Sophie was not there.

The young man went to the foyer hoping to find Sophie with the lady of the house. The foyer was empty.

Hampig checked the other rooms.

In one of the rooms, he found Sophie's mother arranging the furniture.

"Where is Sophie?" Hampig asked.

"I don't know, my son. She might be with the Lady." The mother replied.

"No, she wasn't there." said Hampig.

Hampig murmured to himself, "This is strange!"

Automatically he went to the kitchen. The cook, an elderly hunchback lady, was working.

"Did you see Miss Sophie?" He asked.

"Oh, my son, she might be in the garden."

Hampig took a breath. He pushed the door open and took a few steps down into the garden.

Many a night he and Sophie would wander in the garden. So, she could be waiting there for him.

He looked around, under the trees. He stepped over a few furrows as he looked for Sophie.

He felt his heart beating fast.

"Where could she be?" He murmured.

In the corner of the garden, next to the wall, there was an old, dilapidated gardener's hut.

Driven by an unknown force, Hampig rushed to the hut, pushed open the door and after taking barely two steps, he stood petrified.

In the corner, on a large couch, Sophie was in Dr. Magosian's arms.

For just one moment, Hampig froze, looking at the scene. He then quietly stepped back, opened the garden gate and left.

With his head hanging down, he quietly walked all the way to the mountains.

It was a beautiful sunset in spring. He admired the multi-colored horizon. There was something bluish, sedate, and happy soaring in the air. In the surrounding mist, the range of hills appeared like waves at a distance.

The seagulls hovering in circles were taking their last dip. A sweet and refreshing scent touched Hampig and he sighed, "Oh, what a beauty!"

Then in a reckless manner he jumped down and ran to the bosom of nature... to the only thing that is not deceitful; to the only thing that stays true to the depth of its existence...

***

One morning at the beginning of winter, Ghazar, an old fisherman, and his coworkers were pulling their net. The catch was bountiful! And the fishermen were happy.

Suddenly someone barefoot, covered with shabby clothes and without a hat, jumped into the boat.

The fishermen were amazed; they looked and screamed, "Hampig!"

"Let's haul in the catch," said Hampig and started pulling the net.

"Young man, what happened to 'Madonna'?" asked Ghazar.

Hampig looked at the fisherman, not understanding the question.

"The one who took you away from here; that Madonna," said Ghazar.

"She died," Hampig said calmly.

"May God bless her soul," uttered the old man in a tone of consolation.

And the three of them pulled the net.

LITTLE SEP'S STORY

Under the scorching summer sun, Serko the oyster peddler was carrying an empty clay jug on his head. His bare feet were burned and blistered from the heat. He was sweating profusely. His chest, from under his wet white shirt clinging to his body, was heaving with each labored breath. He was walking from Pera all the way to Chuksaluh.

Walking through Og-Meydan, he cast a shadow on the street which was five times his height. The top of his shadow ended in the shape of a cone, which was due to the jug on his head.

His head, under the weight of the jug, tilted forward, but appeared contented. He was barely twenty-five years old. His large shoulders appeared to give him the power of youth. He was wearing woolen trousers, tied at the waist with a white rope in place of a belt. Covering his unruly hair was an old 'fez' (Ottoman cylindrical red hat), on which he had wrapped a red handkerchief. The triangular end covered his ear and gave him the appearance of a wrestler.

The difficult life these people live at sea and under the brutal sun in the streets seems to give them their strength and energy. In their crude manner, they seem to experience happiness, something that the more sophisticated with their refined and easy life cannot find. I think that God had His hand in this.

Oyster Serko was now climbing up the rocky slope of Ayazmayi with unbelievable ease. He seemed to be deep in thought. His lips were moving – probably without him realizing it- and he appeared to be complaining, "What kind of life is this? Walk all day long; burst your lungs yelling, and sell your produce cheaply...?"

Then, as if struck by lightning, his thoughts stopped and he had a strange look about him, "I wonder what the bitch did?"

He continued walking his path through the narrow alleys of Chuksaluh. He climbed up and down and finally stopped in front of a dilapidated house, the inside of which could be seen from the street. He placed his jug on the floor, took out a rusty key from his pocket, opened the door, and with his jug went in.

It was a frightening experience to see the inside of this house. There was a smell of decay there. There was a cold sensation in every corner, in every object and in everything! To the sensitive eye the ghost of misery made its presence felt - a broken pitcher here, a kettle there, a seared pot, newly washed rags, and over there a bed with a bedspread torn to pieces... Age, poverty, and misery... The entire furniture of the house consisted of a few chairs without backs, a floor mat, small, insignificant things... barely anything!

Serko entered the house overlooking the street and threw himself on the floor mat. He then took out the oily purse that was folded in his belt, emptied the coins into his salty palm, and started counting. "Twenty-six *Ghroosh*" he whispered in contentment. Twisting his mustache he murmured, "So tonight I am visiting Todi."

He was trying to take a nap when a gentle voice from the street distracted him. He stood up. "It must be Sep," he said to himself.

He stuck his head out the window and shouted, "Hey, Sep, where are you going at this time of the day?"

"*Akhpar* (brother), I am not done yet, I am still selling, but there are no customers," the twelve-thirteen year old Sep answered timidly. Sep was a short, energetic, and naughty boy. He wore woolen pants, was barefoot, and was holding two glass jars filled with mussels.

"You son of a bitch! You didn't sell your mussels? Go, go to hell! Come back in an hour with your mussels sold; otherwise I'll smash your skull."

"Very well, *akhpar*," said the boy as he glanced secretly at the smiling face appearing at one of the windows of the house.

"Sep" was short for Hovsep or Hoosep. Hopping and skipping, he ran down the street yelling in a melodic tune,"mussels, mussels…"

Serko, looked after his brother and whispered, "I'll teach you a lesson, you bastard!"

***

An hour passed. Serko slept well. Little Sep came back with empty glass jars. He had sold everything. He was jumping up and down while humming the tune of a playful song. He approached a window of the humble dwelling, placed his jugs on the floor and, hanging from the ledge of the window, he pulled himself up and looked inside. Satisfied with what he saw, he came down with a wry comment, "He is totally asleep."

Slowly he snuck over to the next dwelling and with a soft cowardly voice, said, "Aroos, Aroos…"

117

His call was more effective than an official announcement. Immediately responding to the call, a little girl's smiling face appeared - the same face that had smiled at Sep an hour ago. She had beautiful green eyes and pale lips. The mark of misery and starvation was imprinted on her face.

The youngsters' eyes met in a warm embrace. They were looking at each other in a more than pensive manner - Love...

"What were you doing, Aroos?"

"I was sweeping the floor, *akhparig*," replied the little girl with a sweet voice full of coquetry. A voice that is born in every girl and grows and gets more intense with age. "What did you do?" she asked.

"I sold mussels," replied Sep, tapping his pocket so that the jingle of coins could be heard.

Aroos held her skinny arm out of the window and lightly caressed Sep's long hair. Sep lowered his head. He took pleasure in the caress and let Aroos continue.

Suddenly he raised his head and asked, "Aroos, what did you eat today?"

The young girl trembled and a blush spread over her cheeks. Without looking at Sep, she said in a low voice, "dry bread."

Sep's eyes clouded; a faint sigh emerged from his throat. He looked around, then slowly dipped his hand in his pocket, took out something, and placed it in Aroos's palm and whispered, "Buy some honeydew tomorrow, OK, pretty Aroos?"

Aroos was deeply touched; she didn't withdraw her hand; it was as if frozen there.

"Keep it, keep it." said Sep hurriedly, "it will fall."

He had barely finished speaking, when a loud voice startled him. Aroos's head disappeared suddenly. Serko, who had just woken, was looking out the window and screaming, "You bastard! I'll break you into pieces. Come on in! Come on in!"

The poor boy gathered his jugs and in dread and fear entered through the door that his brother had opened. Serko grabbed Sep by the ear, twisted it, and struck Sep's face with two severe slapping blows.

What a heart-rending scene!

"You bastard!" yelled out Serko. "Haven't I told you a million times not to mingle with those low-life people? Don't you remember what Mom used to say: 'You have to answer to me the rest of your lives if you talk to those people; they gossip about us and nip at our flesh all day long?' Think! If Mom saw what you were doing, she'd curse you forever. Look at me!" continued Serko while shaking little Sep's shoulder. Sep was staring at him scared to death. "If I ever see you do that again, I'll break your neck. Do you understand what I am saying? Now, go and complete your chores!" He pushed little Sep, who fell on the floor without making a sound.

"Oh, I just remembered," said the rascal, this time in a milder tone, "Where is the money for the mussels?"

Sep stood up; his head bowed down, and handed the money to Serko, who immediately started counting.

"This is twenty Ghroosh short. Look in your pockets again."

"No, brother, that's all," answered Sep in a trembling voice." I had to sell it at a lower price. Fifty para is all of it."

"A~h!" Mumbled Serko frowning." I am yet to make a man out of you."

He put on his cloak and shoes and stepped out, saying, "If anyone asks for me, tell them I am at Todi's."

When the sound of his footsteps disappeared down the street, Sep stood up, rubbed his burning eyes and murmured, "She had eaten dry bread... Oh, poor Aroos!"

***

After that incident, Sep was very careful in meeting Aroos. He was fearful of his brother's punishment. In the mornings, when he went to sell the fish and mussels, he would sneak a look at Aroos's window. A game of hide and seek would take place, and both youngsters were happy.

They didn't know why they loved each other. They had grown up in poverty and poverty still surrounded them. Maybe that was the reason that these young ones, who were of the same age, had a hidden love for each other- an innocent and pure emotion which was blossoming.

Sep would take advantage of his brother's fishing trips and sneak into the neighbor's backyard, which was separated from theirs by a meter-high wall. They would perform some plays: "visiting guest," "baby-baby"... and once they played "wedding game." They even touched their heads just as is done during wedding vows. Aroos's grandmother, looking from the second floor window, whispered, "God willing"... while sewing a garment.

Every night, Serko would come home drunk. Along the way, he would have unkind words for everyone. Most of his curses were directed at the "neighbors next door." Then he would turn on Sep, who hid his fear and hurt. Sometimes Sep would attempt to answer or confront the brutal nature of his brother, but then looking at his own fragile body, would come to his senses and avoid any confrontation. He would swallow his pride and anger. All that he could think was, "if only I grow up."

***

Winter had descended with white, shiny crystals. Winter was like an ornament, with cotton-shaped flakes. It covered the cracks in the houses and the dirt in the streets, things that otherwise appeared ugly under the rays of the sun.

It was the Saturday before Easter. Early on, with daybreak, Serko was separating his mussels according to their size: large, medium, and small. Then he would arrange the fish. He would caress them with satisfaction and would take the largest one in his hand, and as if weighing it, would say, "This is great..."

After finishing his arrangement, he went and kicked Sep, who jumped out of bed. He had worn his clothes to bed because of the cold.

"Hey," said Serko, "take this basket. See that you don't sell a kilo of *Kefalin* (a type of local fish) for less than five *Ghroosh*. That's all I am telling you. There are three kilos here, which makes fifteen *Ghroosh*. After you finish your sale, bring the money to me at Todi's. If I am not there, hurry on home. Did you understand me, thick head?"

Without any comment, Sep put on his shoes, put the basket on his head, and left. As he passed the neighbor's house, he looked up and whispered, "Aroos, tonight I'll get you fish."

He walked down the snow-covered street shouting his sales call.

The snow became more intense and the flakes were large. There was no wind. There was a total silence in the streets of Chuksaluh. Night had fallen. Darkness, without being noticed, was progressing along with the flakes of the snow. Little Sep, with his hands in his pockets and his thin shoulders bent forward, holding the handle by his teeth, was running past the houses. He opened their door, pushing with his shoulder, entered the house and looked around in fear, "He is not here. What a relief!"

He went down the stairs and found himself in a dark square place, which could have been a kitchen. He listened attentively; there wasn't a sound. Driven by his inner emotions and his cold-stricken hands, he removed one of the bricks on the floor and took out a pot. He replaced the pot and the brick, and then opening the garden gate and ran out.

There was a fish weighing one kilo. He placed the basket on the floor and went to the partition and yelled, "Aroos, Aroos." Aroos's pale face appeared at the window. Sep said, "Come on down."

A moment later, leaning over the barrier, Aroos was smiling at the plucky boy, who was staring at Aroos in amazement. Next to where they were standing, there was a half-covered well.

The snow was falling on their heads and cloaks as if it was trying to cover a sad and miserable thing.

"Is your aunt here?" asked Sep.

"No, she has not yet returned. She took her weavings to get her money."

"How about your Grandma?"

"She is asleep."

"Look, Aroos, I brought you a fish." He showed her the plate, in which the fish was covered by snow.

Aroos was leaning over more; Sep was standing on his toes. They could feel each other's breath.

"Do you have oil to fry the fish?" asked the boy.

"No, we don't."

"Oh, how about coal?"

"No, we don't."

"Oh."

Sep searched his pockets and took out a forty Para coin. He put it in Aroos's hand and said, "When your Grandma comes, give her the money. Let her buy coal for you."

They were gazing at each other in a loving manner, driven by their mutual misery. The scene being displayed by these two youngsters was very touching. Aroos was leaning over the barrier. Sep was extending his arms and wrapping them around

Aroos's neck. He was softly kissing her cheeks... They did not feel the cold or the snow. Nothing...

All of a sudden, thunderous footsteps interrupted this beautiful scene.

Serko, like a depraved beast, was running in the garden yelling, "You bastard..."

The entire episode was so sudden and shocking that little Sep was shaking and Aroos, losing her balance, tumbled and fell down into the well without making any noise.

This whole thing happened in a second.

Serko was running after Sep, shouting and yelling, falling, getting up and running again. -He was drunk- and more vicious than ever. Sep was running in circles in the garden, screaming and crying, "Aroos fell in the well... Aroos fell in the well..."

Taking advantage of his brother's fall, Sep ran to the well and shouted, "Aroos, Aroos..." There was no response; he repeated the call... no response. He bent over the well screaming and yelling desperately.

In his state of despair, he hadn't noticed Serko, who had gotten up and had reached him. Serko kicked Sep in the back. Sep let out a large, painful scream which disappeared with him falling into the well.

What went through the mind of that enraged drunk...? He was shocked. He held his head in his hands and beat himself in the face and the chest. He cursed loudly and threw himself into the well.

***

The snow was falling heavily. Like a shroud it covered the fatal site as well as the traces of Sep's and Serko's footsteps.

If one had passed by the garden a half hour later, he would have admired how the snow covered the entire backyard like a blanket.

123

ARDASHES HAROOTUNIAN

1873 - 1915

"One has to do what others have not done."

Harootunian

ARDASHES HAROOTUNIAN
1873 -1915

BIOGRAPHY- He was born on October 3, 1873 in the village of Malgara. His education was interrupted. He left school to work in his father's shop. He never left Malgara. He contributed to the newspapers in Constantinople.

LITERARY ACCOMPLISHMENTS-

Poems *Lkvads Knar* (Abandoned Lyre), 1902; *Yergoonk* (Conception), 1906, and *Nor Knar* (New Lyre) 1912. In his autobiography, he says, "I have a fourth book of poems which I have labored over for several years." Unfortunately, there is no trace of that. He has used the pen name Garo.

Literary Critique- His critical evaluations put Harootunian in a class by himself. Keen, sharp, and super observant, he was an evaluator of literary works. In his *Timasdverner* (Silhouettes of Portraits, a series of articles), he presented almost all of the major writers of his time in an eloquent manner.

Short Essays- A collection of short essays.

PENNAMES- A.H., G., Garo, Har. Ard., Malgaratsi, Malgaratsi Garo, *Manishag* (Violet), *OOrvagan* (Ghost), and Shahen-Garo.

LITERARY CHARACTERISTICS-

He is known to be a sharp and meticulous literary critic. His critical evaluation of literary works is a unique contribution to Armenian literature. His command of the Armenian language is immaculate. Although self-taught, his knowledge of world literature and contemporary philosophy is outstanding.

MY LONGINGS

There are longings deep in my heart
That destroy me day after day.
Like the bright red flame
That consumes the candle wax.

Longings are set deep in my heart,
That shatter me day after day.
Like the red flames of burning light
That consume me without delay.

There are longings in my brain too,
Probing my mind day after day
'Wonder if aches like this will die
I ask myself in silence and awe.

The wound gets deep day after day
As longings persist and never die.
I am the coffin of misery and pain,
That no one will ever know.

MY GRANDMOTHER'S DEATH

(Excerpt)

I loved my grandmother and had the utmost respect for her. She was a lady of relatively large frame, slightly hunchbacked, with calm and determined moves. I had always known her as an elderly lady with a large black veil covering her forehead in a triangular manner. She had lost her teeth a long time ago and because of that, her delicate lips were drawn into her mouth and her pointy chin was tilted upwards getting close to her nose. In her little hazel eyes, there were dreams, sweetness, sadness, and discreetness. She had a self-assured determination, though not imposing, but never yielding. Her skin was white and on her soft cheeks there was a tint of redness. Against her wrinkles and nature's attempts to disrupt her harmonious appearance, she always had a delicate face and a tender skin. She must have been a beautiful girl in her youth. I had known her for more than thirty years, but I had never witnessed an incident that would mar her harmonious behavior. She had always been the loving, impartial, never-boasting lady. She had not attended any school, but she was not like the "normal" old ladies.

The year she lost her husband, she also lost her eighteen year-old youngest son. This was a severe blow to my grandmother and she sank under a very heavy burden. This lady could not find solace for years; unfortunately she was not a naïve believer either and for years she couldn't even laugh. When people would try to console her, she would sadly smile, as if telling them that they couldn't understand the pain of a mother. Only her oldest son's wedding restored her happiness. Her joy was her grandchildren, whom she used to coddle on her knees. Her daughter had children too. Grandmother loved them

129

all equally, but she got solace from her son's children. She had one son left, and that was my uncle, who at age fifty became ill. He went to Constantinople, but sadly didn't come back. I was told the sad news and I was entrusted to inform the old lady and my uncle's family about his passing.

How would I do that? I reluctantly became a liar; I concealed the news. Suspicion was thickening in the house but I would fake letters to dissipate the mood.

My grandmother was getting very agitated; she was anxiously seeking news even from flying birds.

A week passed and the news arrived.

My grandmother squatted on the floor, with her veil on her shoulders; she was beating her chest and with subdued voice would murmur incomprehensible words and cry. Ironically no tears would flow down. Once in a while she would say, "My love, my son, why did you take my heart? What am I going to do now?

All that was left for me to do was to deeply respect the moment. I withdrew to a corner, held my tongue, and committed to silence.

After that, my grandmother lived for about a year and a half, I believe merely to be with her orphaned grandchildren. She got ill but refused to go to doctors. "My sorrow has shattered me; what would medicine do to me? All is gone..." She had clearly decided to die.

She was in her shrouds when I visited her. She didn't have the appearance of a dead person. Her eyes and mouth displayed an eternal peace; there was a smile on her face; her silvery hair was like a crown around her head. She didn't have the look of struggling with the angel of death; she was at peace.

CONTRADICTIONS

I and others.

I have been unable to solve this mystery. To forget oneself would mean to forget everything. To forget oneself would mean to be adopted by the great absolute unknown... and after that, be nothing! I would remember others in me as they march on the platform of my soul's theater performing the comedy of existence. The universe shatters in the prism inside me; that is why it exists only because of me. If it has a subjective existence outside of me, what meaning and significance would it have without me? What help would its chaotic, unformed, and useless reality offer? The world has a meaning only because of me. The rest is falsehood and fiction or a painful delusion. I have found more selflessness in those souls that advocate selflessness. Their individual praise of their souls is a glorification of those of others. Whether they know it, or not, is immaterial. After all, all souls are temporary players in this world. That's it! Let them do whatever they can. And this, really, is not a gift.

IN CONTEMPLATION...

Those who are unique, are not necessarily superlative; but they do attract attention.

The literary style is not an ideology, it is not the result of ideologies either; it is the person himself.

Love is the rebirth of life.

ROOPEN ZARTARIAN

1874 - 1915

"The judgment of the mob is the philosophy of the street."

Zartarian

ROOPEN ZARTARIAN
1874 – 1915

BIOGRAPHY- Roopen Zartarian was born in the province of Severeg. The family moved to Kharpert (Harput) in 1876, where he was a student of Tlgadintsi. From 1892 to 1903, Zartarian taught at the *Azkayin Getronagan* (The National Central) School of Mezre. He was arrested in 1903-1904 and accused of political activism. After being released, he went to Manisa, Izmir, where he taught in the local schools. He moved to Plovdiv, Bulgaria in 1904, where he published the *Rrazmig* (Combatant) newspaper. In 1909, after the proclamation of the Turkish Constitution, he returned to Constantinople.

On June 1910, he started the *Azadamard* (Freedom Fighter) newspaper, which he continued until his death in 1915. The newspaper became a hub for articles about nationalistic and artistic issues. He was elected a Delegate to the National Assembly of the Armenian Church.

He was survived by his son Hratch Zartarian, a well-known novelist in Paris.

LITERARY ACCOMPLISHMENTS- Roopen Zartarian started writing at the age of 17 and contributed to Chobanian's *Dsaghig* (Flower) Newspaper. A prolific writer, his contributions are in the following genres:

Fables and Myths- *Karatsadsner* (Turned into Stones), *Dsovagin Harsuh* (The Mermaid), *Ov vor Sultan M'ooni ir Hokiyin Mech* (Whoever has a Sultan in his Soul), *Zarnvads Vorsortuh* (The Wounded Hunter), *Prrnavorin Artsoonkuh* (The Tear of the Oppressor), *Yotuh Yerkichneruh* (The Seven Singers).

Poems and Free Verse- *Menavor Dsarruh* (the Lonely Tree), *Kamprruh* (The Mastiff), *Leran Yeghnigin* (To The Mountain Deer),

Pakinin Parrapanootyoonuh (The Glorification of the Temple), *Jakharagin Kertvadsuh* (The Mill's Poem), *Kyooghin Kerezmanotsuh* (The Cemetery of the Village), *Tashdayin Verchalooys* (The Sunset of the Fields), *Garodner* (Longings), and *Poghotsuh* (The Street).

Novels and Novellas- *Sev Havuh Ganchets* (The Black Hen Called), *Nahanch* (Retreat), *Abreloo Hamar* (In Order To Live), *Dan Seruh* (Love of the Home), *Sareroo Dghan* (The Boy of the Mountains), and *Zghchoomuh* (Regret). A collection of his verse appeared in his book *Tsaykalooys* (Dawn) in 1910.

Literary Critique- *Vaghva Kraganootyoonuh* (Tomorrow's Literature), 1900; *Tlgadintsi*, 1908; *Avedik Isahagiani Abu Lala Mahari Panasdeghdsootyoon* (Avedik Isahagian's Abu Lala Mahari Poem), 1910.

Textbooks- *Meghraked* (The River of Honey), a series of six volumes for primary schools, 1911 – 1914.

Translations- He has translated from the works of Maxim Gorky, Percy Shelley, Victor Hugo, Oscar Wilde, and Anatole France. His own work *Tsaykalooys* was translated into French and published in Paris in 1912. Alongside the *Azadamard* and *Pakine* daily papers, he published weekly periodicals with the same names.

PENNAMES: *Achk Yehovayi* (Jehovah's Eye), *Aslan* (Lion), The Correspondent, *Ezhdahar*, *Hay Aksoraganuh* (The Armenian Exiled), Hratch, Hratchya, R.Z., Shahrooman, Zarman, and Zartar.

LITERARY CHARACTERISTICS- Zartarian is recognized as an unmatched fable writer in Western Armenian Literature. With his symbolic fables, he invented a superb and unique artistic form. His descriptions of the beauty of his native land are like masterfully executed paintings. His symbolism runs deep into the psyche of his people. His style is unbound and his language flawless.

THE WOUNDED HUNTER

A.

A wild buck is running on the mountain jumping over impassable rocky paths, where only snakes can roam. He leaves behind drops of blood on the rocks that he crosses; the blood is fresh. His horns topple down unstable stones from the rocks that he touches. He gushes over boulders frightening baby doves from their nests and muddying the pristine waters running down the mountain. He is running fast; his heart is beating fast; he is frightened.

Down the mountain, at quite a distance, a man appears with a quiver on his back; his bow is taut. From that distance his arrow will not reach its target. Boulders and bushes are obstacles; only lizards can crawl up; one has to be like a snake to climb.

On the misty mountain range in *Masdarra*, a buck runs chased by a hunter.

B.

In the mountains, beside hazel and mulberry trees, thousands of flowers grow, blossom, and perish. Mint also grows; shrubs kiss the ground and the sounds of brooks disturb the silence. There, in the valleys and caves, does give birth to their offspring. The buck's offspring graze at high elevations where there are pointed rocks.

The buck is the offspring of the mountains. The huge boulders have molded him and the mosses that he feeds on have nurtured him. Masdarra has given birth to the bucks; damned is the one who shoots them!

C.

The buck ran away with the hunter following him.

But there are no pathways; one has to have reptile's feet to climb up. The hunter went up and up tracing the drops of the buck's blood. He walked up and up not realizing that the mountain leads to death, that there are no paths for return. He who shoots a buck is damned to die.

He reached the top, but there was no buck! Did the rocks hide him in their crevices, or the caves in their gulches? Who knows! The hunter looked and looked and couldn't find the buck. Enraged, he smashed his arrow pouch, his bow and arrows... the pieces scattered in the wind.

Here and there eagles were screeching, flapping their wings. In their aeries, rotted bones and unrecognizable bodies were scattered. Pieces of clouds appeared and started moving out.

Fear crept into the brave hunter's soul, who was all alone on the mountain. His uncertain footsteps disturbed him.

D.

Climbing up is easy, but coming down is treacherous. He had forgotten the path he took; he couldn't find safe spots to step on. It has been said that the hunter of a buck is damned and his death is a torment. One cannot see the downhill path of a mountain, and plummeting down leads to the most horrific demise.

In desperation, he looks at the thinning horizon, which now caresses the mountains. A faint hope seems to appear; he shouts; he pleads in a shrieking voice. The echo of his voice spreads and reverberates in a devilish way in the rocks and boulders. The calls of deer and the sounds of wild animals seem to spread in the cool shadows of the night.

He is standing alone atop the mountain, his hair waving in the breeze; blood oozes from his bare feet. He is hopeless; he cannot go down! He is waiting for someone to come. Only grasshoppers fly by in groups and dance down the mountain joyfully. He follows these creatures with envy. Once in a while a tumblebug passes, disturbing the silence.

He stayed there, on top of the mountain, waiting anxiously for someone who would come. Death came and sealed his eyes in their pouches and cast the head on his shoulders.

The mountain has a song now: damned is he who shoots a buck!

THE KAMPRR

(An Armenian Shepherd Dog)

Kamprr is grand and majestic. He is nourished and grown strong by the invigorating breeze of the fields. He walks with victorious and calm grandeur when the city-dwelling horde of timid, skimpy, and blabbering dogs attempts to chase him. His curly hair covering his sides is a sign of the nobility of his breed. Yet, the hair on his back has thinned, pointing to his struggle with age and his sterility. His strong chest bulges forward, giving him an extraordinary overall beauty; it separates him from the rest of the dogs that breed and grow in muddy and trashy sites – those are the pathetic ones that are running after him and barking at him.

Why do they bark? It is vulgar passion, which arises from the grime of the streets; an impulse to counteract the insult of inferiority, in order to establish relative respect. As a result, the dogs roam in the streets yelping. They come, one and all: those lying in front of butcher shops and bakeries with their useless offspring. Others inform their comrades at the slaughterhouses to come to their aid. The elderly brag in husky barks. The younger ones threaten in ridiculous tones; and the little ones, driven by the attitude of their elders' audacity, curse in reprisal with their immature voices and run after *Kamprr,* who, with splendid confidence, continues his path.

The multi-voice, multi-language clamor spreads like a storm, but it does not shake the confidence and bravery of *Kamprr,* who happens to have caused all this fury, disturbance, and unrest. He walks; only once in a while does he turn his head and look sternly at the most fiery ones, who have dared to come too close to him and whose breathing he feels on his curly tail. He doesn't growl at the detestable, filthy, and brazen-faced wave of attacks, nor does he address the creatures.

This incompetent persecution of the pompous, filthy mob is pathetic. On the other side, a display of dignity from *Kamprr,* who, unfortunately is limping now because of an injury to one of his front legs, which effaces the wholeness of his looks. But that injury, rather than affecting his grace and self-esteem, gives him more grandeur; it enhances his power and self-reliance.

What had caused this anomaly to leave the mountains and come down to the plains and from there to the city? What kind of luck has brought him to this foreign land, where he joins his hungry brothers roaming around in the rain and sleeping in muddy waters?

Here, his own offspring, not used to this type of lifestyle, wouldn't be able to survive; they would be begging to get a piece of bread. What is this sad reality of animals' submission to survival, which is so much like humans' instinct for indispensable things?

If he can't tell his story, his limp is a vibrant attestation to it.

It is apparent that this nomad is a member of the community. The *Kamprr* was born to brave parents; he spent his youth in the hazards of the mountains; he had committed himself to hating wolves and protecting herds. He had witnessed his mother's revenge against the damned wolves; her passionate and heroic bloody struggle; he had seen how far the protection of the herd can go. Everything should be sacrificed to secure the trust of the shepherd. If required, one should die in front of the shepherd and the flock as a sign of devotion.

That's how the dawn of his life had begun. After that, one miracle followed another. How proud was the mother, when one night she came home from a glorious fight her face covered with blood. Her young son, the *Kamprr,* like the cub of a lion, had displayed his unbeatable strength. That night, the mother rested her head on her paws and slept comfortably, because her cub's hoarse barking was rumbling in the valleys and gorges and that kept every single wolf trembling in his den.

Years passed and the same lifestyle continued with the same zeal and unrest, without any weakness or hesitance. But merciless time with its satanic aging process crept up the mountain and found him. His hair started shedding; the rich curls started losing their curves; the hair on the back started thinning, leaving the skin exposed; and in his last fight, one of his front legs was injured irreparably. He felt something was crumbling inside of him. His limp was an obstacle now for his zeal and it would hinder the use of his strong chest. Furthermore, the admiration that he used to get from his master had now changed to pity; the environment was also losing its charm because of his hopelessness. His inner pride and stamina couldn't accept all these changes. He didn't want to submit to humiliation; he wanted to cast off this condemnation.

And so, weary and tired, he started limping down the slope of the mountain to the plains, ending up in the city. Here, in the streets, where unworthy dogs of all breed and color run after him, barking at him and challenging his courage and power.

This world where dogs live is pitiful; there is so much commotion for a piece of bone. Is a bit of bone in these filthy streets that precious, that dogs fight even with cats to grab a piece, and some of them dare to display their grinding teeth?

Stupid animals! Rise above your skimpy environment. Rise above your pathetic shallowness; try to understand the magnanimous feelings of *Kamprr*. Fill your hearts with his nobility. Then and only then will you see the bottom of your pathetic lives. Who are you persecuting? What is the cause of the frenzy of your barking? Is it that difficult to see his magnificent posture, his beautiful pose and his imposing wholeness? *Kamprr* walks calmly, without hurry, courageously and in self-confidence ignoring the pack of dogs and leaving behind the deafening screams of those pompous dogs with their threatening barks.

The judgment of the mob is the philosophy of the street which declares its greatness; it consists of hungry dogs, deprived offspring, and a canvas of blind puppies.

Walk! Hold your head high, oh, *Kamprr!* Walk through these mediocrities! Leave this ludicrous arrogance behind you; arrogance that doesn't feel ashamed to bark at magnanimity, that screeches against dignity. Arrogance that wants to expel you from these sites, so that it can dare wiggle its tail for a piece of bone. Walk along this road to the end! You have come to the wrong place. Go back to the vastness of the plains, to the seditious mountains. It is better to die hungry than to extend your legs begging for a piece of bread. It is better to be wounded and die in an uneven bloody fight with a voracious wolf than squat on a corner in these streets and die slowly, ending the part of life that was blessedly granted to you.

THE VERSIFICATION OF THE SPINNING WHEEL

Autumn nights are long and life freezes outside. With the first call of the roosters, the spinning wheel restarts squeaking in the house, under a gloomy ceiling. It is the melody of the ruined house on the street of the desperate ones. It is the saddest of all melodies emanating from the fingers of the old lady.

The flickering clay lamp resting on the window sill brightens the desolate room and the spinning wheel; there the old lady, with her bad eyesight, is bending over the wheel and is rolling the yarn that is churned out. She is all alone with her memories. The wheel turns and laments the fate of the cotton-yarn. Through two meager tear drops falling from her tired eyes, she looks at the present. Far away on the horizon, a window is opened, through which she recollects the entire path of her life's journey.

Like a young boy staring at his reflection in a lake, she too is trapped in her dreams of the years passed - a young girl, the only sister of many brothers, the most lovable and favorite of her mother and father; her engagement and tender love; then the adoration and suffering of motherhood, tears and happiness; the growing up of her children and later her getting old and facing deprivations - the entire untold emotions. But these are deceiving, games that memories play. Her lost days are actually her present reality- she is not old, she is not alone, she still has her stamina, her loved ones and old times...

She turns the spinner along with her sad memories. Her shadow, displayed on the wall, ridicules her moves.

Hours pass. The awakening signs are heard -a baby in a crib longing for her mother's milk, the tolls of the church...- The spinner stops. The old lady makes the sign of the cross and heads toward church to request the belated death to knock on her door, to turn out the lamp which has ran out of oil and would not be refilled, and which flickers but never glows.

INDRA

(Diran Chrakian)

1875 - 1921

"All big things are controlled by small things."

Indra

INDRA (Diran Chrakian)
1875 – 1921

BIOGRAPHY- Diran Kasbar Chrakian was the second son of the Chrakian family. He was born on September 11, 1875 in the district of Uskudar, Constantinople, Turkey. The Chrakians were migrants from Dikranagerd (Diyarbakir). He attended the district's Mgrdich Arrnavoodian's *Soorp Khach* (Holy Cross) primary school (1881-1885). He then attended the Berberian School (1886-1891). He was accepted at the Painting Department of the Aesthetic School of Constantinople. He didn't graduate. It is said that he "couldn't tolerate the rules imposed there"; however, he continued painting on his own. In 1888, the world-famous Armenian-Russian painter Hovhanness Ayvazovski visited Constantinople, where he admired and praised Chrakian's paintings. Chrakian contributed to *Serve tee Finoon* periodical with figurative paintings. In 1897 his family moved to a new house, where he met and fell in love with Verzhin, his future wife, to whom he devoted pages of literary masterful pieces addressing her as Irena. On July 3, 1897, Chrakian went to Paris to further his studies in the arts, but did not meet success there. He moved to Geneva and later, at his friend Michael Gyoorjian's invitation, went to Alexandria, Egypt in September of 1898. He began writing a "diary of meditations about gloomy moments," which became the basis of his most celebrated masterpiece, *Nerashkharh* (The Inner World). His father died in 1898 and he returned to Constantinople, where from 1898-1915, with minor interruptions, he taught in Armenian schools, including the famous Berberian School. In 1899 he married his love Verzhin, (whom he referred to as Irena in his *Nerashkharh*). In 1913 Diran and Verzhin had a son, named Vren. During this time, the first signs of spiritualism appeared in Diran's life, when he met Seventh Day Adventist preachers. From 1914-1918 he served in the Ottoman army as a translator and a clerk. During these times, he faced some difficulties: he left his family, burnt his handwritten manuscripts, and became a preacher of the Seventh-Day Adventist denomination. He was imprisoned several times and, in 1921, arrested and accused of sabotage activities against Ottoman Turkey. He was exiled from Konya to Diyarbakir, where he died on July 6, 1921. (Details of martyrdom on page 33.)

LITERARY ACCOMPLISHMENTS-

Prose- *Nerashkharh* (Inner World), written in 1900 and published in 1906.

Poem- *Nojesdan* (Cypress Groves), a book of poems, basically sonnets, published in 1909.

Literary Criticism- He has also written literary criticism and philosophical essays, which are dispersed in the newspapers of the time.

PENNAMES- Dion, Diran, D.Ch, and Indra.

LITERARY CHARACTERISTICS- *Nerashkharh* (The Inner World) is a prose-poem, one of the most unique literary works of the century, and one of the most beautiful displays of the Armenian language. It created turmoil in literary circles, however. Chrakian had to write many critical essays evaluating and explaining his own work. Chrakian describes his Inner World as the "union of philosophical and aesthetic modes."

He stands alone in Armenian literature for creating multitudes of new Armenian words; he is daring and ignores grammatical constraints when constructing Armenian compound words. He is in the modern Armenian vernacular as Naregatsi was in the classical Armenian literature.

Ardashes Harootunian's review: "Nerashkharh is a description of the exceptional behavioral moments as exhibited by the human soul. It is poetically spirited and emotionally lyrical. It is a tempest; an uncontrolled tempest, where incompatible and diverse emotional states are displayed. It is an utterance and hallucination of an explosive emotional rage.

"Nerashkharh is a site of magical visionary moments. It is where reality and imagery collide in confusion. The images and events are dream-like and abstract, at times unrelated and unbound. It does not satisfy the tendencies of the real world.

"Nerashkharh has no confinement; no scale of coherent reality, it is unique and remarkable. The abundance of images are intermeshed and display rich colorful moments.

Nerashkharh gives us the poet, the lyricist, and the artist."

TRANSLATED WORK

IRENA

My personification, my idealized ether, my nocturnal, let me possess you, let me be ecstatically and euphorically elated by you. You are the enchanting pure melancholy that calms the cries of my troubled tranquility. Aren't you my eternal right? You are the whole that my being is part of; my divine existence, my soulfulness. Shouldn't you blend with me, liquesce with me, have no other life but that of my ego, no other form but my soul, no other place of existence but my infinite annihilated space? Come back to me, you, who are born from my blood, my thoughts, and my imagination. You, who like a cloud of incense, were taken from me at times unremembered. I know you! Do you think I have forgotten the adoration I held for you during my ecstasies? You were the embodiment of my prayers. Do you think I can forget my existence? Do you think the withered rose doesn't recognize its oily sap or the orange-blossom its birth? I

149

have panted only for you; I have existed by you; I understand only you. You are my breath and my sap. I want to mold with you and be part of you. You, my contentment and my holiness. Kissing your lips and before bursting into auroras and states of trance, I want to inhale your spirit and feel you with utmost adoration. You are my existence and my ether! I want to plunge in and get high by the scent of your mystical essence; tremble in your blissfulness and fall into a euphoric state. Let me disappear in your truthfulness. Is it possible that my fingers have touched you? Is it possible that I have heard your voice? Have I inhaled your breath and scent? Is it possible that I have kissed your mouth? Please, forgive my miserable longing and my aridity. You are my insatiable happiness, my insatiable freedom, and my deliverance. Have I really kissed your purple mouth? Oh! Please forgive me if by touching you I have turned you into a being. Let me adore you; let me breathe you and come to life as the emerald comes to life by the rays of the sun; as the cypress tree breathes in the night to come to life. Oh, how sweet are you! Your sweetness drives me into melancholy. You are as sweet as rekindled memories. I love you for rekindling my memories eternally; I love you as if you are dead. Once I glanced at your hand. It had a strange appearance: pale and stonewashed. It was as if tinted with a light-green hue, like alabaster covered by shadows in a forest. I didn't know what to make of it. My tears blurred my vision, and then streamed in a ray of light. That was the abstract idea of you which floods my soul. Did you recognize it, my angel? I am smiling thinking that you are unaware of my doings – standing beneath your lit windows at night. Do you know, at nights, I covertly stand in the deserted streets and look at the glimmer emanating from your windows? I feel ashamed to admit that I stand there – not to see you – but to feel you; to admire the light emanating from your window. Then I go to my unhappy room filled with cypress-tree aroma. Shall I tell you, my angel, what I do there? I kneel, I cringe, holding my head in my hands and resting on my bed, I think of you. In the surging glows of light in my mind, I call you. Engulfed in emotions, I choke in the sufferings of knowing you. In the frantic celebrations of your acquaintance, my heart pounds painfully. Beseeching, I think of you. What do I ask of you? Nothing, nothing! – I ask for my eternal dissolution, my vanishing, my consummation, my dispersion, my demise – and in contrast I ask for your emergence, your effusion in the vastness of my nihility. I beseech you... Do I know what I beseech of you?... I beg of you... My beloved soul, trembling and breathless, I want nothing from you; I cry so you exist. That's what I pray, kneeling – and I don't feel any pain in my knees, or in my head, or in my chest. Does my prayer bother you? Do I violate your freedom by calling you in my loneliness and my anility so you exist in my dreams? Do I disgrace your virginity by calling your image in my pathetic male way? Does this really tarnish you, my glowing soul? You, who are the essence of light, born by my tears, by the trembling of my tears, you who are the poem born by the morality of my tears. You and your body are not a thing, but a soul, my soul. My suffering and my destruction, the hampered calls erupted from my inside, from you; pieces from my existence make your existence; make your wholeness. A broken string from my soul adds to the admirable harmony within you. Your heavenly admirable peacefulness arises from my confusion. The more I gasp for air, the more you become soulful. The more I loose and quench, the more you blossom; the same manner as my autumn dreams of your spring; the same way as my putrid self, augments your scent. You are the blissful life of my expiry. Aren't you the heavenly-scented flower on my grave?

151

SIAMANTO

(Adom Yarjanian)

1878 – 1915

"Oh, Human Justice, let me spit on your forehead!"

Siamanto

SIAMANTO (Adom Yarjanian)
1878-1915

BIOGRAPHY- Siamanto was born on August 15, 1878 in Agn, Western Armenia. He attended the Nersessian School in Agn. His father was a merchant. In 1891 he moved with his father to Constantinople, where he attended the Mirijanian School in Kumkapi, then the Berberian School of Uskudar. He went to Geneva to study agricultural science, but realizing his real love was literature, he left the college. During the Hamidian pogroms of 1894-1896, he left Ottoman Turkey and stayed for a short while in Egypt. He moved to Europe, living in Geneva, Paris, Lausanne, and Zürich. While in Paris, he audited literary courses at the department of literature at Sorbonne University. In Europe he had contacts with Armenian political figures and intellectuals, as well as Armenian Students Association, an organization that was disseminating awareness about the atrocities back home.

In 1908, when the Union and Progress Party ousted Sultan Hamid, Siamanto returned to Constantinople; after two years, he left for the United States, where he urged Armenians to go back to their historic lands. He became the editor of the Boston-based *Hairenik* newspaper. In 1911 he returned to Constantinople.

To better know his nation, in 1913 he travelled to Tbilisi, Baku, and Etchmiadsin, and visited the historic sites in Armenia.

Along with the Armenian writers and prominent national figures and community leaders, Siamanto was arrested in April of 1915 and taken to the infamous Ayash prison, after which he was exiled and martyred in August of 1915 in Engyoori, Turkey.

LITERARY ACCOMPLISHMENTS-

Poem- He is the most influential and dominating epic poet in Armenian literature. His first poem, titled *Aksorvads Khaghaghootyoon* (Exiled Peace), [later republished in titles: *Mahvan Desilk* (Vision of Death) and *Godorads* (Massacres), was published in 1898. From there on, Siamanto published *Vaghvan Tsaynuh* (Sound of Tomorrow) in Manchester Paper. His early poems appeared in *Anahid, Panper,* and *Azadamard* newspapers.

His publications are the following:

1902- *Tyootsaznoren* (Epic Poems), which established him as the poet of ideologies.

1905, 1906, 1908- *Hayortiner* (Sons of Armenia).

1907- *Hokevarki yev Hooysi Chaher* (Chandeliers of Agony and Hope).

Play- In 2000, some variants of his poems were found, along with two drafts of an unfinished play. I took it upon myself to combine the two drafts and directed a staged reading of the work in New York City.

Quite a number of his works have been translated into Russian, French, German, and English.

PENNAMES- Abbasian, A., Abbasian Arsham, Adom Mirza, Harootyoonian Jack, and Siamanto, A. Y.

LITERARY CHARACTERISTICS- He is one of the most influential figures of Armenian poetry. Siamanto does not write about his personal feelings. He has no personal love poems; his world is the world of the collective Armenian engulfed in atrocities; his work is an expression of the reality of revolution of his time. He is the observer and the echo of the massacres of 1896. He did not live to witness the 1915 massacres. One can only imagine what he would have written had he survived to witness them.

He wrote about Armenian heroes, who had shaped the Armenian Identity. His poem about St. Mesrob Mashdots, the inventor of the Armenian Alphabet, is a masterpiece.

He contributed to shaping the free-verse style. He invented many new compound words, which helped him expand the expression of ideas and sentiments and brought a particular flavor to his symbolism.

With strong national convictions, his poetry became a string of deep emotions.

He is the master epic poet of his generation.

TRANSLATED WORKS

STRANGLED

There were forty of us in an underground ditch.
Like a herd of horrified cattle persecuted
By the blows of a howling sandstorm,
Huddled together and trembling in fear of an imminent death,
We were submerged in the total darkness of four walls.

A colossal horrifying silence was pressing upon us!
  -No whispering, no breathing, lips were sealed-
Our evil and awful gaze was a wish of death for one another.
From dawn to dawn,
Hungry and silent like the stones of graveyards,
We clenched the colossal horror on our bodies like an iron cloak.
To shatter our hidden anger and longing,
Most of us started biting our fingernails in a rage,
While the unbound silence, like eternity, covered our eyes.

But out there, under the sun, thousands of barbarians like animals,
Not tired yet of destroying fertile fields and villages, they were
Searching for our hiding place, anxious for our demise.
In the darkness of the ditch,
With imminent death hovering upon us.
It was with horror, horror, horror,
That we heard the crackling noise of rifles, daggers, swords
And spears like the roar of thunder under the sun.
Quivering bodies, bodies, bodies, like uprooted trees,
Were falling on the roof of our ditch.
Their sighs of death, at times faint, at times loud,
Creeping through the walls, were driving us to insanity.

Then, through the cracks of the ceiling logs,
Resembling the shutters of a coffin,
The profuse warm blood of the dying found its way through
The cracks and drop by drop dripped on our faces.

Right then a newborn baby started to scream.
This poor innocent baby undoubtedly
Was about to be the informer.
A decision -a death sentence -a crime- was our last hope.
When the sobbing mother finally whispered,
"Lord, have mercy upon us. My breasts are dried-up,
I don't have a drop of milk I fed him my blood,
I don't have a drop of milk... decide what you may..."
"He should be strangled." said one angrily waving his arm.
"He should be strangled." all forty of us whispered in unison.
"Strangle me first then my child."
"They heard the cry! They are digging with shovels!"
"We are all doomed! They are digging the roof already!"
"Dirt is falling already! Light is shining already
Through the ceiling!"

"I beseech you, strangle me! Here is my neck
And the neck of my baby…"

And in the dark, the Armenian mother offered her
Neck and the neck of her baby.
In total darkness, two arms, swirling like snakes,
Found the baby's neck and vehemently strangled it.

Now, the silence in the ditch was like a tempest.
I thought all of us had died deservedly.
A moment later, the deceived, hopeless and blood-thirsty horde
Departed shouting vulgar curses.
Was this salvation for us?
Do slaves have salvation?
Is this the way to be saved?

And every day now, that poor woman, wrapped in rags,
Standing on the streets, clings to strangers,
Passersby, foes and foreigners, and in a rage of insanity,
Screams frantically, "These hands do you see?
Do you see these hands?
I was the one who strangled my newborn in the ditch
With these hands.
Believe me, it was I who strangled my baby.
What kind of cruel people are you?
At least strangle me! My hands are too weak.
It was I, in the ditch, who strangled my newborn
With all my strength.
Don't you have a heart?
Strangle me!
My hands are too weak…"

THE DANCE

Suppressing the tears in her blue eyes,
In a field of ashes, where Armenian lives
Were still being slaughtered,
This is what the witnessing Fraulein told us of our horror.
"This unbelievable story that I am telling you,
I saw with my own merciless eyes.
Safe in my room, looking through my window,
Grinding my teeth in formidable anger,
I watched hell being played out in the field.

"It was in the City of Bardez, which had been burnt to ashes.
The pile of corpses reached to the top of the trees.
The bubbling sound of the brutal revenge in your blood
Running through the rivers, springs, streets and homes,
Still ring in my ears.
Do not be horrified by this story!
Let men know man's crime against his fellow man.
Life is short. En route to the grave, it lasts only two days
Under the sun, and yet man commits
Crimes against his fellow man.
Let the conscience of the world know this!

"That deadly morning was a Sunday,
A useless Sunday rising over the corpses.
All night long, leaning over a stabbed maiden in my room,
With tears in my eyes, I was trying to console her last moments.
Suddenly a bestial mob appeared at a distance;
Pushing and whipping twenty brides and chanting words of
disgrace. They stopped by a vineyard.
I left my poor maiden in her bed and approached the balcony
Of my window of hell.

160

"The bestial mob grew in numbers.
A ferocious man screamed at the brides,
'You must dance; you must dance to the beat of our drums.'
The whips started lashing fiercely at the Armenian brides
Who were longing to die.
The twenty brides holding hands started a circular dance.
Tears were flowing from their innocent eyes.
Oh, how I envied the beautiful wounded Armenian maiden in
My room, who gasped her last breath cursing the universe
As she softly released her dove-like soul to the stars.
Clenching my fist, in vain I gestured towards the mob.
'You must dance!' The mob was shouting furiously.
'You must dance until you die; you pretty infidels!
You have to dance bare-breasted,
With smiles on your faces and with no complaint!
Tiredness and shame are not for you!
You are slaves and you have to dance naked and exposed.
Till death, you must dance, seductively and invitingly,
We are thirsty for your moves and your death...'
The twenty brides fell down exhausted.
'Rise! Rise!' shouted the mob, swirling their swords in the air.
Then someone brought a canister of kerosene to the mob.

"Oh, justice of humanity let me spit on your face!

"The mob anointed the twenty brides with kerosene.
'Dance! Here is a fragrance that even Arabia doesn't have.'
Someone lit a torch and set on fire the naked brides.
The seared bodies embraced death through dance.
Horrified, I slammed shut my windows like a tempest.
I approached the lonely, breathless maiden in my room and
pleaded, 'Tell me, how shall I gouge out my eyes?
How shall I do that? Tell me!'"

THE DREAM OF THE BRIDE

"Alone for years. Sitting at my window now,
I am gazing at the road of your return, my beloved wanderer.
With this note, once again, I would like to hum
The orphaned trembling of my body and my thoughts.

Do you remember how bright the sun was
On the day you departed?
Its glare was as plentiful as my tears and as hot as my kisses.
It was as kind as your promises and as swift as your return.
Do you remember the sun and my prayers
On the day of your departure?
I sprinkled a jug of water upon the shadow of your horse,
So that the seas you were to cross would contract
And the land under your feet would blossom.
Alas, that sunny day turned into a dark night.
And under the burden of mounting years,
Tears flowing down my cheeks, like falling stars,
Withered the roses in my heart.

It is enough!
I want to pluck my locks to quench my thirst for you.
I am still drunk from sipping your glass of wine.
I am mourning the absence of your elegant figure.
Immersed in your memories, I am sighing with the winds.
My knees are bruised from kneeling at the gates
Of the church beseeching your return from the West.

Let the seas dry up from shore to shore,
And for a moment, let the continents adjoin.
Then I won't need paradise or the sun.

Come back!
Standing in my black dress at the doorsteps of our home,
My hands deprived of yours,
I wait for your return.

Come back!
Like the sweet fruits of our garden,
My love is preserving its kisses for you.

My milky-white body has not been blessed by motherhood.
I have not been able to decorate a cradle
With my gold-ridden bridal veil,
And I have not, I have not sung
The pristine heavenly lullabies of Armenian mothers.

Come back! My longing has no more heights to climb.

When darkness arrives by unraveling its shrouds,
When owls mourn each other in the yard,
When my sobs fade and my tears turn into blood,
I, lonely in my abandoned bride's dreams,
Like a demon, with my hands
Will sprinkle my imminent grave's soil on my head."

A HANDFUL OF ASHES

Alas... you were magnificent and grand like a palace,
And I, atop your white roof,
Filled with hope under the star-studded skies,
Was listening to the gushing sound of the Euphrates.

   With tears in my eyes, I heard that they crushed your huge
   Walls, one-by-one, and scattered the debris on the flowers
   In the garden surrounding you.
   On a bloody day, a day of horror; a day of massacres.

And the blue room turned into ashes.
The room, where I spent my happy and joyful childhood
On the carpets behind the pillars,
And where my life and soul had soared high.

   Did the gold-framed mirror shatter too?
   The mirror, in whose imaginary space
   My dreams, hopes, affections, undeterred will,
   Along with my thoughts, had reflected for years.

And the singing fountain in the yard, did it die?
Were the willow and the fig tree destroyed?
And the brook that once ran through the trees,
Did it dry up? Tell me, where is it? Did it dry up?

   I often dream of the cage by the roses,
   Where my gray dove used to carol every morning
   As I would wake with the rising sun,

My paternal home, believe me, after my demise,
My soul as an exiled dove,
Will roam over your darkened ashes

Crying and lamenting with songs of misery.

> *But, who will bring? Tell me please,*
> *Who will bring a handful of your sacred ashes*
> *To sprinkle on my remains in my mournful coffin?*
> *I, the songster of my Fatherland.*

A handful of ashes on my remains, my paternal home.
A handful of ashes of your ruins, your memories,
Your grief and your bygone days.
A handful of ashes to sprinkle on my heart...

A NIGHT OF REST

All night long I attended the sick.
Piously, I lead all the wandering blind men
In the forest to the marbled temple.
***
The convicts are wandering in the desolate garden
> *Tolling their chains under the moon.*
They are longing for running rivers
> *And fields that are waiting to be reaped.*
They are thinking about mothers who are making
> *Wreaths and lanterns for them...*

Far away, by the banks of a river, they nailed several
> *Coffins with the eternal golden hammers of insanity.*

And I guess all the sisters of mercy, gathered under tents,
Are sewing white linens, on this rainy night, for the wounded,
Who are sleeping side-by-side and staring at each other.
A flock of lambs passed through the fog
And are exiled to the slaughter house,

Along with the screams of dismembered, innocent
        And bright children.

My friends picked poisonous flowers
        To decorate my faraway gravesite.

On a stormy night, I shook the hand of an enemy in a
        Friendly gesture,
            Before kissing a girl stricken with tuberculosis.

Oh, I will put out my lantern now.
I will hurriedly close all the shutters of my windows,
So that I do not hear the mocking laughter of the crows, which,
in their death-boding flights,
        Penetrate my soul tonight.

And tomorrow, before dawn, you and I
Will sail the river filled with blood.
To what destination? I don't know!

Maybe there, where you and I, and all of us
will find a place to rest...

MY SOUL

And now, the torches of my soul brighten my thoughts
        Every moment, after drowning them in total darkness...
My soul has lived all of your miseries thousands of times.
My soul kneeling on its own ashes in a valley
Laments my dear sisters, who are exiled in chains.
My soul is the place wherefrom a blood-ridden moon
Rose on fields filled with massacred innocents.

My soul is the gale-stricken forest, where my brethren's
Blood flows around its ponds.
My soul is the nation, where flocks of dark-haired
Orphans run through ruins escaping
The persecuting shining Daggers.
My soul is the sky, wherefrom the stars of hope fell down.
My soul is the marble cathedral, where life is kneeling
Eagerly begging for the most merciful death...
My soul is a gospel, where pale and hopeless hands
Flip the pages in vain seeking the impossible atonement.
At times, in my soul, mornings are stained with blood,
And an unspeakable symphony of beseeching cries erupts.
There is a world of slaughter in my soul, where horrified
Lives are waiting for your help, your move and your voices.
In my soul there is the birthing of heroes
And the marching of corpses coexisting side-by-side.
Today, my soul is like the rain falling on skinned corpses,
And it is the gaze that penetrates all abandoned coffins.
My soul tonight is a storm of anger and resentment;
Against which all blood-thirsty armies will retreat.
And all the graves, from their depths, in a rage,
Right before your eyes, will stand and stare at the sky,
So that you, unmerciful,
Realize that the martyrs, one morning,
Willingly sacrificed their lives for yours.
My soul is a death-witnessing autumn,
Which spreads the last breath of its dying leaves on everything.
But my soul is a struggling Hopelessness,
Like a prophet, which will march toward the fertile
Death of undefeated Hope.

THE CRY OF THE LAND

(Excerpt)

"If you want your ancient nation to survive,
If you want your homeland not to crumble on itself,
If you want me to give birth again to heroes of freedom,
If you want my horror-bearing rivers not to be swamped with
    Corpses,
If you want my stars to sparkle and my fields to flourish,
If you want my springs to radiate like dreams,
If you want my plains to become oceans of wheat fields,
If you want my motherly milk to irrigate your vineyards,
If you want my dawns to rise with shining suns,
If you want my valleys not to sob under the shadow of death,
If you want my generations to flourish,
    And for at least one morning, a smile to be born on my face,
If you want peace to live permanently in your homes,
If you want the warm blood of your children
    Not to flow over the rocks in my paths,
If you want your Revenge to be fulfilled
    And your Hatred satiated,
If you want Justice to be established and its capitol erected,
If you want Haygashen*, Armavir*, Dikranagerd* and
    Ardashad* to be born again,
If you want your souls to be strengthened and your
    Pride restored,
If you want the harsh morality not to dig new graves
    Before you,

Then come to me, furiously and in regiments,
With your arms extended to the iron clasps of mutiny
    And facing off all tremors.
Shout out loud your whole-hearted and furious Hatred

Against the deadly crisis that is bound to fall on these days!
Call out loud for a triumphant armament: bravery,
    Irrevocable rebellion and hope!
Call out loud like the uproar of thunders – everywhere
    In the fields, in the cities, in the souls!
For I know after these decisive engagements,
You will be erecting on my forehead, by your own hands,
    Monuments built of my enemies' bones.

With all your spirited anger, cry out for help!
Let the crowds of all my dispersed Armenian children
Come together, be brothers again,
    And be inflamed by the lethal calls of your revenge.
Let your wrists strike like lightning,
    Your minds be satiated with blood and hope,
    And let your swords flash in the air
    With the emitted flames of your horses.
Let your torches spread out like suns
    From one battlefield to the next,
    And from one summit to another.
I beseech you, rush to help! Rush to help! Rush to help!
For the love of my children, and for the sake of securing
    The rise of future dawns.

And in order for your souls to be valorous
    And your postures defy reticence,
And in order for Hatred in your hearts
    To be profuse like the sea,
And in order for your paths to be decided,
    And your will turned into a storm,
And in order that the death of your nation - at least
    Once- pierces your brain like a dagger,
And in order for your wrists to strike

169

And your torsos harden like metal,
See for once, the caravans of my forgotten children
    Beseeching for help-
See their bodies, which have been devastated by the
    Crimes they faced,
And their orphaned souls wounded by your negligence,
And their haste to climb upward the impassable routes
    Of exile of my hills,

Look at their terrified glances in response to imminent death.
Hear their prayers, cries, and implorations.
Again and again, filled with hope and expectation,
    Addressed to you, my distant, exiled, persecuted children,
They are expecting from all of you in a brotherly manner a move
    Of protection or a drop of blood,
    Fortified with fighting souls and hope.

Hurry! I am addressing you!
Because all lives will be destroyed.
All couples will be widowed and all men will perish.
Unknown to them, all the newly born babies, in the
    Folds of their bloody swaddles will open their eyes in death.
And all corpses in their shrouds will be dismembered
    And be stabbed once again.
All the fertile fields and golden crops will be burnt to ashes.
Hurry! All the steeples of cathedrals will crumble.
All cities and villages will disappear under the collapsed
    Ruins of centuries-old fortresses.

Hurry! My brave and revengeful children,
Go to your sacred land bare-breasted with your lances raised.
Put forth your armors to the winds of battle swirling
    Your weapons.

Hurry! Move ferociously with the vengeance of a tempest
*   To my impregnable and eternal terrains.*

Let me tell you this, my hesitating children,
It is only after vengeance and resentment
*   That the saintly and heavenly Love of Life*
*   Will live in my colossal motherly bosom.*
Because, alas, I am the only one who witnessed how
*   Flooded blood shook the seven foundations of my existence.*
I am the only one who knows the repeated terror of
*   Crepitation of the half-opened coffins, piercing my soul.*
Only I heard the unspeakable roar of the dying...
The outcry of those who wanted to be saved,
Their painful pleas to live to see the sun, the sun.
Only I witnessed the anxiety of the lovers
*   Who adored each other*
*   And the lamentation of widowed mothers who were*
*   Separated from their children.*

Along with that, I heard the horrific sound of the
*   Grinding of bones, and the decapitated heads from*
*   Guillotines plummeting on my forehead.*
At last, I only witnessed -for a long time now- only the
*   Piling of skeletons in the crevices of my heart;*
*   They multiplied and perfused like forests.*

And now, all of you, who have adhered to my body and Soul,
You, the Faithful, you the Pilgrims,
You my innocent dear Ones,
You, who shared my pain and shed your blood without
*   Reservation for me,*
You, who did not fall for desertion's vices,
I am addressing you.

Be strong! Be hopeful! Bless yourselves with the cross!
Because, brothers who are conscious and regret their
*   Evasive attitudes are coming back,*
Miraculously stripped of Hatred and filled with Love,
And through the blaze of dawns to come
They extend their strong hands seeking yours. "

* *The capital cities of historic Armenia.*

[Note: The Armenian Apostolic Church believes in the miracle of the invention of the Armenian script. Siamanto has devoted three poems to the inventor of the Armenian script:

- *St. Mesrob,* an ode to the Saint;
- *The Prayer of the Saint-* where the Saint is beseeching God for help; and
- *The Vision-* St. Mesrob's vision, where a Hand inscribed Armenian scripts on the wall of his secluded hermitage.]

THE PRAYER OF THE SAINT
(Excerpt)

"Grant me light, oh, irrefutable God,
The inexplicable architect of the universe,
The creator of fate and cognition,
The tempest of breath, central authority,
I, Mesrob, the servant of your holy altar,
Beseech you to grant me clarity
For my hazy vision.

Help me, oh, boundless Knowledge,
Almighty Father, eternal creator,

The zenith of light and bright wisdom,
Heavenly cleanser and the soul beyond universe,
The unbound grantor, the giver of abundance of dream,
Let the bright cover of your Knowledge
Wave upon my wrecked shoulders.
And tonight, oh, immutable and unbound God,
Let your creator's hand,
On the fortieth night of my vigil of sighs and prayers,
Let it touch my brains and mold my invention."

THE VISION

You are the miracle; you are the glow of the intangible
*   Faith*
You are the astonishing power,
You are the burning talisman, you are the mysterious
*   Sacrament,*
You are the angel in Mesrob's dream.

With your luminous right hand,
In a sacred moment,
You etched the letters of the Haigaznyan* nation
On the walls of his hermitage.

Suddenly, the Saint, inspired by the vision,
Stood up as if from a grave,
Took his feather pen and a board,
Kneeling under the vision
Wept for the miracle of the Vision.

* Haigaznyan- Refers to Armenian nation.

173

KEGHAM PARSEGHIAN

1883 - 1915

"Heroism is born through labor's misery and will power."

Parseghian

KEGHAM PARSEGHIAN
1883-1915

BIOGRAPHY- He was born in 1883 in Constantinople. He attended the Armenian National School in the Gedig Pasha District. Later the *Getronagan* (Central) high school. He studied sociology and political science in Paris, and did his apprenticeship in journalism at the *Menzume* newspaper. He was on the editorial board of the *Soorhantag* (Messenger) and *Azadamard* (Freedom Fight) newspapers. From 1909-1915 he was the assistant editor of *Azadamard*. He and Shavarsh Misakian published 41 issues of the *Aztag* literary periodical. In 1914, he, Hagop Oshagan, and Gosdan Zarian published *Mehian* (Temple), a literary periodical.

LITERARY ACCOMPLISHMENTS- He wrote numerous editorials.

Short Stories- *Abarrni Kaghakin Khoozargichuh* (The Inspector of a Future City), *Sbasooms Gakhaghanin Vra* (My wait at the Gallows), *Misian Gooka* (The Messiah is Coming), *Aysbes Badmets Vrizhapip Azadootyoonuh* (This is how Vengeful Freedom Told the Story), *Tsyoonamrriguh* (The Snow Storm). In 1931, the Friends of Martyred Writers in Paris published his collective works.

PENNAMES- Kegho, Ned, Oshin, Oshin-Zartonk, Parseghents K., K., K.P., Vahakn, Varaztad, Zartonk.

LITERARY CHARACTERISTICS- In Western Armenian prose, Parseghian was the first to describe the life of laborers. In allegorical writings, he dealt with the will power of humans. He has also described the atrocities of the Turkish Government.

Pareghian's prose has the quality of poetic free-verse. He portrays his heroes with such vivid imagery and detail, that one could paint from his writing. He writes in an unusual dense form; nothing extra. His works are poetic pieces.

A NEW YEAR'S TALE

The little one's mother had died, but he didn't know she had passed away.

His bigger sister had told her that mommy had gone to some faraway place and will return with red and blue toys, money, and clothes.

The sister would go on, that mommy will be back the following day in a car, dressed in a shiny dress.

The little one had looked at his sister's face and smiled. The sister too, had looked directly into the little one's eyes and she too had smiled. But when the little one cried, the sister hugged him and lifted him up and kissed him, and kissed him until the little one had smiled again and had wrapped his little arms around her neck.

The following day, the little one was sitting at the window looking outside; he was waiting for Mommy. After all, the big sister had said that Mommy would come bringing red and blue toys, money and clothes.

- Mommy will be back today, right, sister?

- Of course, she will come riding in a car with a colorful dress.

And the little one would joyfully wait.

- Where is she? It is night already.

Night had fallen. A big noisy car came and stood in front of their house.

A majestic, beautiful lady, with earrings and a necklace, exited the car and went directly into the opulent house across the street. She was carrying a lot of boxes.

178

The little one left the window; lying on the floor and covering his eyes with the back of his hand, he was crying; Mommy was going to come, but did not.

He was crying copiously.

The big sister picked him up again, hugged him, and took the little one's curly head into hers.

His crying subsided and quieted down.

Why do you cry, my love, said the big sister, Mommy will come the day after tomorrow with lots of red and blue toys, money, and clothes.

The little one quieted down again and rested his curly head on his sister's bosom.

He started playing with his sister's hair, then walked around her and left. He cried again and laughed again. Came and curled up in his sister's lap and slept.

Days and nights followed each other. The little one was sitting at the window looking for the car that would bring his Mommy.

A beautiful car came and stopped in front of their house. The majestic and beautiful lady, with earrings and a necklace, stepped out of the car, looked at the little one, didn't smile and went into the house across the street. She was carrying boxes wrapped in green and orange gift papers.

New Years arrive with beautiful cars but they don't stop at the nests of poverty, where people await expecting cajolery.

THE HUMBLE HEROES

... Sparks fly in darkness like metal rockets or fountains of fire; they are plentiful; glowing, they fall down like rain in the darkness of the miserable factory.

Hammers, in revenge, strike anvils with roars and thunder with the full force of the laborer's arm until the sharpness of the piece is shaped.

...Aware of their harsh deprivations —and yet full of pride - the laborers are unyielding in their exhaustion; and if they are miserable and unlucky in their lives, they are determined to crush that misery with the sounds of their hammers, which along with their willpower molds the nails. The flashes of the sparks light their faces as if to canonize their ignored and forgotten heroism. It is through misery and the willpower of labor that heroism is born.

The mallets of the laborers strike again and again. Sparks fly and their faces glow in darkness.

THE ACCIDENT OF THE LITTLE WORKERS

Ardash and Karrnig are two little boys who come from poor families and are working in a bookbinding factory.

- My back, my back hurts! I am so tired.
- I am tired too; my arms are aching.

Their voices, merely a murmur, were drowned out in the corner of the large room, under the scrunching noise of folding large papers and the deafening noise of the machines.

They had started work in the early hours of the day. All day long, with their small bodies and hands they had folded papers and worked on cutting machines. It was evening now, but they had not yet finished their work yet. They were trying very hard to finish up the day's work with the last bit of energy their feeble bodies could muster. They were waiting for the night to fall so they could go home. What happiness that entailed; their tormented bodies and limbs would, at last, rest a bit.

Their work was so arduous and painful. But who could they complain to? Who would care to listen to the complaints of these young laborers? In their ignored, despised, forgotten status, the young boys found solace in sharing their concerns and worries with each other.

Ardash and Karnig were too young; eight or nine years of age. Their young bodies needed a healthy, nourishing environment to grow properly. But deprivation had hounded them down mercilessly. They were deprived of school, affection, and the normal pleasures of life that youngsters of their age are in need of. Playing games and leisure were unknown to them. They didn't have the so-much-desired caring at home either. Their families were engulfed in their own struggle to secure the daily bread, hence didn't have time for caring.

These kids, who were forced to start work this early in life, had become philosophers.

In the morning, having placed a piece of bread and cheese - sometimes just bread- in a small container, they would spring out of their homes. Ardash lived in Uskudar and Karnig in Khas Kugh [neighborhoods in Istanbul]. The kids would rush to catch the first ferry, in order to get to the factory on time. As if the all-day brutal work conditions were not enough, now they had to be there before the doors opened. That was not easy, especially during the cold winter days. The boys would shelter themselves by the door, keeping their hands in their pockets.

It was during this ordeal that the two strange boys had become like brothers. They cared for each other; their friendship deepened; they helped each other; if one of them

181

had any difficulty operating a machine, the other would run to help. They complemented each other's work; they even covered for each other. That was the happiness that they didn't have outside of that friendship. They would share the pain for each other, too. When the boss would land his fist on the head or back of one of them, the other would feel the pain; tears would fall down from their innocent eyes. While other boys would have found solace by going to their mothers, Ardash and Karnig had each other for comfort. In order to dilute the effect of the incident they would rush back to work by folding and cutting the papers again.

That awful cutting machine was the nightmare of all workers.

It was Christmas Eve. Everyone gets ready for something during feasts of this nature. Ardash and Karnig were in a somewhat festive mood also. Not because they were going to get a new pair of shoes or clothes; no, that was out of the question. But they were boys; and boys get into a festive mood anyway. No, they had other factors too. They were going to go to church in the morning and evening; more than that, they were going to get a two-day rest and they would have an opportunity to play with their friends. So they were working harder in order to be able to go home a bit earlier that evening.

Karnig was operating the machine and Ardash was folding the papers. Everyone else was attentively working on his task.

- Oh, my hand...

This screeching scream was heard and Karnig, half-unconscious, fell down. The blade had severed the tips of his forefinger and middle fingers. While the boss was ruthlessly reprimanding Karnig and while other workers had not realized what had happened, Ardash rushed to Karnig, picked him up and started sprinkling water on his face, woke him up and started comforting the boy. Taking him by the hand he took him to a drug store.

As for Karnig, everything had turned upside down. It was not only the pain of his hand, his little mind was thinking about the consequences. What would he do without fingers? How would he go home? What would he tell his mother? What would his mother say, who is already burdened by securing bread for the family? How disappointed she would be! Karnig was scared.

Then he saw Ardash, who was leaning over him affectionately and was following the directives of the doctor. Karnig looked at Ardash and felt the torment he was going through. He recalled their love for each other that had made them brothers. He forgot his own pain and his other worries. His main concern was his friend, Ardash. He realized that Ardash too was under the same fate. The machine that had deprived him of his fingers could do the same to his friend. He felt touched. He stared at Ardash, and with a voice so pristine and with deep emotions uttered in their jargon,

- Ardash, *akhbarig* (brother), when you operate the machine, watch out, don't get too close to the blade...

TANIEL VAROOZHAN

(Taniel Chubookyarian)

1884 – 1915

"Believe me, oh, mothers, for I hear the footsteps of the crimson dawn."

Varoozhan

TANIEL VAROOZHAN (Chubookyarian)
1884- 1915

BIOGRAPHY- Taniel Varoozhan was born on April 20, 1884 in the village of Prking, Sepastia (Sivas). The family moved to Constantinople when Taniel was 12 years old. He attended the *Sakusaghaji* Mkhitarist Fathers' primary School in Pera (1896- 1898) then the Mkhitarist Boarding school in Kadikoy from 1898-1902. The Mkhitarist fathers sent him to the Order's Moorad Raphaelian School in Venice, Italy (1902-1905). After graduation, Varoozhan attended Ghent University, Belgium from 1905-1909. He returned to Turkey and became the principal of the *Aramian* school in Sepastia (Sivas) (1909-1911) then the National High School of Tokat (1911-1912). In Constantinople he became the principal of the *Loosavorchian* Roman Armenian high school in the district of Pera, 1912-1915. He was arrested in 1914 and was exiled to Chankiri, where he was put under house arrest. In August of 1914, he and Roopen Sevag, en route to Ayash prison, were brutally butchered. Shamdanjian, an eye witness, wrote about their martyrdom (Page 31 in this anthology.)

Another eyewitness, Sarkis Srents, quotes Varoozhan's last words, *"Don't console me, I'll die dreaming of my race's future."*

LITERARY ACCOMPLISHMENTS-
Poems- *Sarsoorrner* (Quivering), 1906, Venice; *Tseghin Sirduh* (The Heart of the Race), 1909, and *Hetanos Yerker* (Pagan Songs), 1912. *Hatsin Yerkuh* (the Song of the Bread) was published posthumously in 1921 in Constantinople.

In 1914, he and H. J. Sirooni published *Navasart*, the annual literary periodical. Varoozhan has numerous articles scattered in newspapers of the time about pivotal issues concerning Armenian life.

PENNAMES- Chubookyar Taniel, Molla, T.V., Varoozhan Taniel. He used the last one in French, also.

LITERARY CHARACTERISTICS- Varoozhan's themes are wide ranging and encompass the following: his native land and the Armenian people- traditions, deprivations, convictions, traits, survival, and deep concerns about its fate. He writes about the misery of his people and their struggle to survive.

He is sentimental and shares the agonizing experiences of the deprived; he is stormy when faced with the brutality of the oppressor; he is the bearer of hope and wholeheartedly believes in the bright future of his nation.

He accomplishes all that with a superb style that utilizes both rhyme and free verse expressing them with unique syntax. He creates allegorical and vivid imagery, and contrasts them with live events.

His command of the Armenian language is immaculate; he heavily depends on the classical Armenian; he uses old words in combination with contemporary usage of the language. He is a keen guardian of the language. Most importantly, he combines all of these elements in aesthetic art form.

Varoozhan and Siamanto are considered the most dominant literary figures of the first quarter of twentieth century Armenian literature.

THE RED SOIL

There is a handful of red soil in the saucer on my desk;
It is a gift from the distant plains of the Fatherland.
The person who donated it to me
Thought he was giving me his heart,
Never even realizing that
He was giving me the hearts of his ancestors too.

Silent and in grief I stare at it sometime for hours.
It seems my gaze sprouts roots in this fertile soil.

And I ponder.
May be its crimson color is not nature's erudite gift.
This soil is a sponge for wounds;
It has absorbed portions of life and the blazing rays of the sun,
And as an unprotected Armenian land,
It has turned into this bloody shade.

Maybe its past glory: the sparks of stomping hoofs
In bold expeditions, which once covered Armenian
Battalions with victorious dust, still throbs within it.

In it still lives the unique power that, breath-by-breath,
Molded my life and yours. With a conscious touch, it
Granted us the same dark eyes and similar passion from
The Euphrates; capricious hearts and concealed sites for
Rebellion and lustful love.

Here in this soil still gleams the soul of an ancient hero,
Which had been turned into a clot by the beautiful
Tear of a virgin.

In this soil, there is an atom from Hayg,* a speck of
Dust from Aram** and the guardian pupil of Anania***
Brimming with rays of stars.

There is a nation, an ancient nation on my
Desk, which in the gleaming dawn and under
The innate primal soil, converses with me.

It inspires me! And, like the stars dispersed in the infinite
Blue, it irrigates my soul with sweet sparks of flaming dust.

And then, my senses tremble with profuse shivers,
Which in the furrows of the mind is more
Creative than the love-filled breeze of spring.

I sense the trudging of new memories through my mind
Of bloody souls with their deep wounds;
I sense murmurs of vengeance.

And this soil, this cluster of dust, which I keep so dearly;
More lovingly than my soul would have done,
Had it found my ashes scattered in the wind.

This bantookht part of Armenia, this relic left from
Our victorious forefathers, this talisman, this red gift,
Grips my heart with unknown claws, especially when I am in a
Precious sanctuary of love and smiles, or am leaning
On a book at the majestic moment of creating a poem.
This red soil drives me to weep, to roar, to arm my fist
And place my soul in my fist.

*   Hayg- traditionally the founder of Armenia.
**   Aram-traditionally an early king of Armenia.
*** Anania- a 7th Century astronomer.

A LETTER OF LONGING

My mother writes, "my bantookht* son,
How long would you roam under strange moons?
How long shall I wait to have your tired head
Rest on my warm chest?

"It is enough that your feet,
Once warmed softly in my own palms,
Climb stairs alien and far.

"It is enough that your dear heart,
Nourished once by my milk,
Wanes far from my hollow heart.

"My ardent arms are weary at the spinning wheel
Weaving my shroud, now that I am old.
I wish my eyes could see you again
Then wrap my soul in their darkness.

"I sit in front of our door sad and in misery,
Asking the cranes to bring news of you.
The willow tree you once did plant
Is shading me with its branches.

"I wait in vain for your return every night,
I watch the brave men pass by our door.
The farmer passes by, so does the shepherd,
Lonely I remain, the moon and I.

"I am abandoned in my ruined house,
Longing at times for my grave and always for my home
I am like the turtle whose guts adhere
To its shattered shell.

"Come home, my son, revive your paternal home.
The door is smashed, the cellar is robbed,
Swallows fly in freely in the spring
Through the shattered windows.

"Of the many sheep in the stable,
A brave ram stands alone,
Whose mother as a lamb, -remember my son?-
Ate barley from your palm.

"I feed him rice and clover now -the best we have-
To nurture the lard of his tail.
I comb his soft wool with a wooden comb,
    He is a dear victim.

"When you come home, I'll adorn his head with roses,
And sacrifice him for your thriving life
And I'll have your wandering tired feet
Washed in his blood, my sweet, my bantookht son."

* Wanderer (Other definitions on page 41.)

THE FACTORY GIRL

You pass by my window every morning like a shadow
And my leafless rosebush weeps
Upon your beautiful virgin's braids.

In the silence of the street I hear your footsteps,
And the barking of a dog that just awoke.
Or, in my sleep, I hear your cough
That torments your beautiful chest.

And I ponder – oh, dear sister,
You are sleepless and hungry,
And you shiver from the wind,
On your curls rests the frost
Like sparkling sapphires.

Either your shoes are torn
And water gushes through them freely;
Or a rascal Turk, behind you,
Whistles arrogantly.

And I ponder- perhaps your mother is ill at home,
Perhaps the lamp in your house has no oil,
And you are going to work in the factory
To sustain life and bring light to your home.

I ponder – a maddening wish urges me
To come down, my pale-faced sister,
To come close and kiss your feeble hand
And whisper, "I love you."

I love your sorrow, which is my supreme sorrow;
I love your wrecked chest,
Where love stubbornly persists to sing
Like that of the love-stricken lark.

I love your hunger and your thirst,
And your exhausted bones,
I love your dried-up guts,
The mourning of your hair falling over your shoulders.

I want to hold you in my heart like an exiled dove.
I want to give you my power
And all of the laurels of my victories
And my irreproachable last name.

I want to be the shield to protect your targeted chest
And be the covering veil of your honor
And protect your gender and beauty devoid of a smile
With my granite arms.

I want to grant you what the struggle granted me,
What I acquired in battles,
I want to crown you with my victory laurels,
That are as red as my blood.

So that you will not be pale and starving,
So that you will not cough under the sun,
So that the lamp does not go out in your house,
So, dear sister,
You do not go to the factory anymore!

A PRIMEVAL LOVE

Granny and grandpa, two withered souls,
Sitting in the shadow of an apricot tree,
The delicate flowers of which had crowned the head
Of the young maiden who is now granny.

They tremble intensely like two lovers
Who have suddenly met.
But their canes, lying on the grass,
Are the only ones that are embraced.

They don't have the blazing passion,
Their souls have lost the melody of their kisses,
The flare in their tired bodies
Doesn't bloom like lilacs anymore.

Grandpa's gaze wanes in granny's eyes,
Way before it reaches her heart,
And the warm rays of the sun freeze
*   In their cold chests.*

If they attempt innocent emotional seduction,
Driven by love-enriched springtime's aura,
Their hearts will shatter
Like a crystal abruptly placed in fire.

There are no more roses and flares on their cheeks.
Their love is a sparkle buried deep in ashes,
That dies swiftly in a minute
By merely being remembered.

And now in this night of the spring,
Where the scent of the cinnamons covers the hills,

The moments of their old love-making visit them
Like an old prayer.

And they remember in the shade of
The same apricot tree,
Their first embrace and seduction that have long gone.
They remember their kiss and Granny's scream...
And they smile at each other...

THE PERISHING LANTERN

Tonight is the festive night of victory.
    Bride*, fill the lantern with oil!

It is the homecoming of my victorious son,
    Bride, trim the wick of the lamp!

A cart stopped by the well in the yard,
    Bride, light the lantern!

My son will be home crowned with proud laurels,
    Bride, bring the lantern to the doorstep!

But...

Is the cart loaded with blood and mourning?
    Bride, bring the lantern this way!

My hero son is shot in his heart.
    Alas, Bride, turn out the light!

* Daughters-in-law were referred to as "bride" by the husband's family.

THE MASSACRE

(Excerpt)

A black day.
-That day all the stars dripped poison-

***

Lament! Lament, you unhappy mothers
*   And brides in misery.*
Abandon your laments to the stars,
And lament the slaughtered Dawns
*   Of this gloomy land.*
Let your eyes dry by weeping on the fallen thousands.

This is the last cry!
Let your tormented femininity be crushed in its weakness.
One more sigh, one more teardrop,
It is the last one! This is the end!

Because I see new beginnings in your wombs
*   -New Children will be born-*
In their obscurity they will shape the path for the
*   Lions of tomorrow.*
Their eyes, smaller than yours, will look up to
*   The flood of brighter rays of the stars.*
Embracing the essence of existence,
They wander and grow in the ruins of a future
*   Heritage entrusted to them.*
Their lips will echo the thunderous lightning of your lips,
And will soar high up into the clouds,
To the super-godly sacrament of Armenian blood
Wherein the love of Fatherland
*   Will be the faith of thousands of souls.*

And tomorrow, yes, tomorrow,
Oh, pitiful mothers, listen to me!
From your wombs, they will emerge one-by-one
As great heroes.
They will be giants and the tempest in their hair
    Will shake God in the stars above.
They will soar like eagles
Always ready to face lightning.
They will wear the headbands of freedom
With stars as ornaments instead of beads.

Listen to me, oh mothers, listen to me!
When they harness their horses tomorrow,
And their swords of brass are baptized in Vengeance,
And they roar in the mountains with their enraged thirst
For Turkish blood in revenge
Then at once, all our dead will rise in unison,
To stand upright in their graves,
And impatiently and attentively staring afar
Will await the arrival of the crimson dawn.
A dawn,
The footsteps of which,
-Believe me mothers!-
I DO HEAR...!

BLESSING

Let me place a handful of grain
In your palm, my son,
My brave son! My backbone!
Let your arms be as strong as
Those of twenty bulls.
Let twenty homes be erected by you;
And when you seed ten single grains in the field,
May you reap by the number of the stars.

Let me dash a handful of grain
On your head, my dear grandson.
My dear one, the staff of my life.
Let wisdom bless your forehead,
And awareness rest on your shoulders.
And when you attend your flock,
Let one thousand sheep come to feed from
Your hand.

Let me sprinkle a handful of grain
On your hair, my granddaughter.
The rose of my life, the wreath on my tomb.
Let new tulips unfold on your cheeks every spring,
And new rays gleam in your eyes every summer.
And when you plant a single branch of a willow tree
Under its shadow, year after year,
May you remain as youthful as ever.

Let me sprinkle a handful of grain
In your bosom, my daughter-in-law.
My beautiful child, my love afar.
Let in the furrows of your bed

A full line of grains be born.
And let in the cradle that you sway
Mornings of happiness sleep calmly.
And when you milk forty cows
Let your pails be filled with
Silvery milk and golden cream.

Let a handful of grain fall
On our heads too, my time-worn wife, my dear Anna,
Let the sun of autumn never freeze
In our snowy-white hair.
Let the candle of our night
Never burn out in the pillars of the church.
And when we are put into the grave,
My dear Anna,
Let the soil beneath us
Be a little bit soft.

IN MY FATHER'S PRISON

I was a little boy when I visited you
*   In your dark cell in the prison;*
Mother had taken ill. I was wandering
*   Between the prison and her bed.*

They informed you of my visit.
You came to the iron-bar gate
That blocked our passionate embrace -what a crime-
You were silent and sad.

You were frail and so longing to see sunlight.
Your beard, as if grown on bone, concealed your face. Oh,
*   Father, you were a dead man.*

You smiled when you saw me,
*   But that kind smile was a fake;*
Like a blossomed water lily wrongly placed
On a lake of tears.

From behind the dark iron bars,
*   You stretched your lips to kiss mine.*
Alas, our lips could not come close to touch.
We were like a cradle and a coffin.
Oh, how I wished to embrace you warmly,
Grant you the free world outside the cell,
Flood your eyes with the boundless sky seen
*   Through my own small pupils.*
And to empty into your heart my days spent under the sun.
I wanted to flood your cell with roses of spring
And bury my youth and my future in your cell.

Oh, what a sad hour indeed.
I told you bit-by-bit all the sufferings of our home:
The passing of granny; the illness of mom with her cough
That bursts the silence of the nights.

I told you that owls are dancing under the moon
    On our roof;
That our rose vine withered this year
    From the dry winds of the cemetery.

You were listening with an inquiry of questions.
When suddenly a cruel command,
-A command so evil- came to separate us;
You left without kissing me.

Standing there, gazing at your departure,
    I cried there. Lonely and alone, I cried, Dad.
-A new vengeance was born in my chest-
    The tears in my eyes were the echoes of my heart.

Oh, love of life, honest labor, thorny hearts,
Saintly things all thrown into filth.
They are like collapsed veins
    In the much needed paths of survival.

Along with you, drowned in genocides,
I saw, lilacs and saints of all religions,
And Christs who were spit upon.

THE LAUNDRY WOMAN

She was widowed in the year of the massacres.
Her husband rests in the common cemetery,
And her sweet baby sleeps at home.
    Early in the morning on a snowy winter day,
    Under a smoky lantern in a stranger's house,
    Bending over a washbasin with her sleeves folded
    She launders with her fair-skinned arms.
She is young and beautiful.
Under her cover of mourning, she still has
Passionate eyes secretly fighting grief and patience.
    She has not overcome the motherhood of her virginity.
    Her youthful, tender chest is torn between
    Amorous calls and her baby's cry for milk.
But she washes for the sake of a piece of bread
For her only child
She denies submitting to the future her fresh youthful mutiny.
    She is alone in the damp basement, alone with her grief
    Her hair is in shambles, sandals on her feet
    And two birthmarks on her arm.
Orphaned and captive, `
She is facing the washbasin which rests on a blazing fire
She serves her masters washing their filth in sudsy water.
    While her days are poisoned in the haze of the steam
    And her head is crowned by the nettles from
    Her husband's gravesite,
    Bowing her mourning head she works all day long
    Sweating profusely to secure an abundance of milk.
...And over there, her son awoke, alone in his crib,
He cried and screamed, groaned and cried
And choked on his own tears...

DIKRAN CHOGYOORIAN

1884 - 1915

"Nations cannot be free without revolution."

Chogyoorian

DIKRAN CHOGYOORIAN
1884-1915

BIOGRAPHY- Dikran Chogyoorian was born in 1884 in Gyoomooshkhane, Trabzon. In 1897 he was enrolled in the orphanage of *Garmir Vank* (the Red Monastery). Later, in 1898, he was transferred to the orphanage of Galatia. He graduated from the famous Berberian School in Constantinople in 1907. He taught history, geography, and literature in several Armenian schools in Constantinople. He had travelled through Europe and historic Armenia.

LITERARY ACCOMPLISHMENTS-

Novels and Stories- *Vankuh* (The Monastery), 1914, *Herosuh* (The Hero), 1911. *Hayreni Tsayner* (National Voices); a collection of stories, including *Vankuh* and *Herosuh*, published by Zartarian Bookstore, 1910, and *Jampoos Vra* (On my Way).

Editing- Established *Vosdan,* a quarterly literary periodical in 1911, in association with Michael Shamdanjian.

Translation- Works of Guy de Maupassant, Leonid Andreyev, and plays of Henrik Ibsen and George Bernard Shaw.

Essays- Literary review about Alexandre Shirvanzade'.

PENNAMES- Chadion, D., D. G. Ch., Dikran Ch., Mehegan, X.

LITERARY CHARACTERISTICS- In his novel *Vankuh* (The Monastery), he has delved into the internal turmoil of the psyche, writing about the difficulty of making a choice between a self-imposed commitment (i.e., religious commitment) and carnal desires. Two opposite states, indeed.

He has created superb images, often conjoining them allegorically with psychological behavior. He has kept the balance between the internal and external worlds.

His language is pure and careful, reflecting his concern to use elegant words in his descriptions.

THE MONASTERY

(Excerpt)

The dark massive Monastery sits in a plain that lies on the slopes of a hill. Right in the center of the surrounding walls stands the dome; moss has grown in the crevices of the red brick walls, where narrow windows are protected under curved eye-brows. The bell tower that is resting on the delicate columns is especially beautiful.

What style is this? Who is the architect who has designed the steeples that look like head-dresses?

The Monastery is well built; I would say it is really beautiful! They say the churches of Armenia often resemble each other; their oppressive grayness gives them a gloomy appearance.

The hills lined up beyond the gardens that surround the Monastery are barren now. A writer may liken them to peddlers' camels that are kneeling. I look at the yellowish hue above the dark peaks, which have greenish lines on their shoulders. Deep trenches accompany the foot tracks left by men and oxen. They disappear in gorges, and then reappear again, eventually dying at a point in the slope.

Once in a while, a buzzard soars in the blue skies over the unattractive, desolate hills.

The Monastery is not a place to be amused by. I am content with what I see, i.e., the beauty that canvases the entire place. Beauty should live in the soul of the clergy; in the same manner that our Ancestors were nourished by it. A clergyman, in the state of worst deprivation, should seek solace. Solace is born from the satisfaction of beautiful deeds.

When I pass through the muddy riverbed of a brook, I come across large carts loaded with dry grass and being pulled by oxen and buffalos; piles of dried grass extrude and emit the aroma of tea, which fills the evening air. I inhale and my gaunt chest fills with joy. This is a peasant thing, which reminds me of my childhood.

The carts wobble on the bumpy roads, while the endless monotonous sound of the wheels, like music, fills my soul -a harmony of scent and music. This harmony is like the heavenly will, because its elements are pure and pristine.

I accompany the gentle animals as they go to their stables; then I take off and go to the cemetery lying in front of the Monastery.

On the road across from the little bridge on the brook, I see horsemen galloping leaving behind a dust of clouds; people walking on foot and carts pulling heavy weights. I don't know where they are going, but I envy them...

Night has fallen now. Far away, a strip of dark violet on the horizon is filled with redness, like dripping blood. Above that, gold and purple colors tremble. At the zenith, the azure blue has faded.

I have witnessed magnificent sunsets on oceans and mountains, now I am enjoying it in the plains. It is not unique; but it is something fresh; hues follow colors and the plains start losing their identity under the descending mist.

My mentor Doorinian, a moral philosopher, used to liken mist to doubt. Now I understand him; he had all the right to think so. Everyone under this strange sheet gives something of himself, becomes a doubter. In this world, isn't it better to look at things through mist? And after placing everything in the doubting pan, go out there and smile to everyone in an indifferent manner then question them! My kind mentor, Mr. Doorinian.

It is getting dark. A few stars start blinking above the horizon. The intermittent husky barking of guarding dogs awakens me; I still hear the sounds of sheep in the yard.

I enter the Monastery through the curved gate. As I walk through the yard, I notice the only lit lantern in one of the narrow windows, which flickers and whose rays, create kind of a web-like vision.

At night I retreat to my room and in my loneliness, devote myself to the divine pages of Nareg.

FOR MY MOTHER

Tonight, an old sweet word from the past, like a fire, passes by me and touches my heart.

A sound from the past touches my soul; it is my mother's smile, my mother's smile that is awakened in me. My poor suffering mother, frail and abandoned.

A story circles around my ear with sweet vibrations; it reminds me of my mother's grieving lullaby.

Oh, kind, old song, a saintly fable, how did you join my mother's smile and visit me tonight? I don't know how long I've lived, but I have forgotten her pale face.

How I wish, mother that you could again caress my little palms and smear them with beeswax as you used to do when I was a child.

Now strands of beeswax strangle me every day, and my soul stretches on dark and wet grounds like a wounded reptile.

Oh, how I wish, mother, that the innocent, little, good fairies of the valley would take me on their wings to the world of your tears and hide me there. Now my sinful tears crystallize and burn my cheeks. Now the kisses, like blazing iron bars, scorch my face... and see, mother, my heart is a desolate place.

How I wish, mother, to have been a child again and lain, and died under your motherly hugs and tears...

OUR POWER

(Abridged)

Shooshan and her sons were considered rich people in the small town. They were deprived of nothing. Her sons were married. Happines reigned in her home. "Glory to God, glory to the Creator," she murmured. She felt a painful affliction on her face. It was the Event, her life's starting point. She started remembering her prosperous small town, which was turned into ashes... she remembered the uproar, the sounds of hatchets, the fire in the fields and, oh, the blood gushing from severed ears, breasts, and arms... She remebered how a Turk was drinking blood... and another was chewing on a piece of breast. She remembered her husband's last kiss and later his mutilated body... she rememberd the man, the executioner, who struck him with his scimitar shouting, "Die, *Gyavoor* (infidel), this is what Armenians deserve." He had a large scar on his forehead...

Years passed. Shooshan had to work hard to earn a living and bring up her sons. What a joy it was to dance at her son's wedding. What a joy it was to attend to her grandchild. There was a knock on the door. Shooshan opened the door to find a beggar standing there- "a piece of bread for my sons, *Hanum* (lady), we are starving". Shooshan stepped back; she recognized the stranger...

Shooshan ran inside, got the bread, and handed it to the beggar, who left blessing her for the good deed.

Shooshan shut the door.

He was her husband's murderer.

ROOPEN SEVAG

(Roopen Chilingirian)
1885 - 1915

"People are strange, when they come together, they become other people."

Sevag

ROOPEN SEVAG (Roopen Chilingirian)
1885 - 1915

BIOGRAPHY- Roopen Sevag was born on February 15, 1885 in Silivri, Turkey. After the local grammar school, he attended the American Secondary School in Bardizag. He then moved to Constantinople and attended the Berberian School under the tutelage of one of its most famous educators, Retteos Berberian. He graduated in 1905. Upon the recommendation and with help from the principal, Mr. Berberian, he attended the medical school of Lausanne, Switzerland. After graduation in 1911, he practiced medicine in Lausanne, Switzerland from 1911-1914. He married Yanni Apel, a German girl, and had two children, Levon and Shamiram. In 1914 he, along with his family, returned to Constantinople. Prior to WWI he was called upon to serve in the Ottoman Army as a physician. The godfather of his children was the famous musicologist and composer Gomidas Vartabed.

He was arrested and exiled to Chankiri. Being a physician, he attended to the daughter of Cheteji Arabaju Ismail, who had suggested that if Sevag converted to Islam and married his daughter, he would be saved. Sevag refused adamantly. He and Taniel Varoozhan were martyred on August 26, 1915. Ironically, the day following their murder, a pardon was issued for Sevag. (Details of his martyrdom on page 31).

LITERARY ACCOMPLISHMENTS-

Poems- His first poem, *Pazhanman Khosker* (Words of Parting), dedicated to his principal and recited at the graduation, was published in Masis Periodical in 1905. During his lifetime, Sevag published one book, in 1910, entitled *Garmir Kirkuh* (the Red Book), which contains three poems: *Charti*

Khentuh (the Madman of the Massacre), *Turkoohin* (The Turkish Girl), and *Marterkootyoon* (Song of Humanity). He has numerous poems published in the literary newspapers in Constantinople.

Chronicles- *Puzhishgin Kirken Prtsvads Echer* (Pages Plucked from a Doctor's Diary, *Siro Kirkuh* (The Book of Love), *Verchn Hayeruh* (The Last Armenians), *Kaosuh* (The Chaos). His collective works were published posthumously, 1986 and 1995.

PENNAME- Roopen Sevag.

LITERARY CHARACTERISTICS- Sevag's thematic spectrum is very wide. He has touched upon the themes of love and nature, as well as social, humanitarian, and national issues. He is very courageous and robust in his approach.

He started out with poetry, with rhyme and rhythm. His prose is multifaceted also. Being a physician, he tackled many social issues: prejudices, deprivations, bad behaviors, and mass indifference.

The 1909 massacres of Sultan Hamid had a large presence in Sevag's poetry.

He is very conscious of the language he uses: pure and pristine Armenian.

This following poem, along with many of Sevag's nationalistic poems, was the reason for his arrest, as he was accused of being an instigator of nationalist tendencies in Armenians.

The Madman of the Massacres was written after the Adana massacres of 1909 by Sultan Hamid. The first staging of this poem was done in 1958 in Baghdad, Iraq. The piece was also presented in 1965 in NYC. Both were staged under Herand Markarian's direction.

THE MADMAN OF THE MASSACRE
A Monologue

The Bursting Laughter
The Roaming
The Red Judgment
The New-Comers
The Old Priest
The River
God
A Song in the Night
The Crime
The Vow of the Race

(The Madman enters bursting with laughter)
Ha, ha, ha, ha...
Here I am roaming in the silent fields of the slaughtered,
Carrying my father's corpse on my shoulder.
You senile priest! Your pitiful corpse is so heavy,
So very heavy on my shoulder...
You expelled me from my native nest, as if I were mad,
You didn't think at all that I would return to find you
Strangled like a dog in your damp hideout,
And offer you my debt, my last debt.

(Bursts with laughter) Ha, ha, ha, ha..
Here they are, all the wise men,
All of the intellectuals of this stupid world,
Who roamed around dragging their lethargic souls

And counting their beads of fortune.
And once every Sunday, fully-fasted,
With heavenly devotion, kneeled in front of Madonna,
Offering candles...
Then to adulterate, to lie and to pillage
All week long, without fear or concern.

(Laughs) Ha, ha, ha, ha...
Here they are, all the feeble-minded choristers,
Who ridiculed every challenging question,
The cheap sophists and shallow philosophers
Of the Psalms,
They would have convenient solutions to harsh issues;
Sitting under the Sword of Damocles,
They would steal and fill up their granaries for wedding
Celebrations to come,
Without even thinking about death.

(Laughs) Ha, ha, ha...
But why does my laughter tremble so much?
Here they are, all of them... all of them... all
In the darkness and abyss of silence,
Lying senselessly, lying unholy,
Lying eternally in boulders of pain and agony.
Lying... Oh, my Lord,
And they are so many, so many they are!
Spread out to the edges of distant roads,
Like the copious post-flood forests.

(Bursts with laughter) Ha, ha, ha...
In the silence of the night
I hear the crushing sounds of cracked bones

In the jaws of howling dogs...
Friendly dogs, friendly hands,
Friendly tongues licking open wounds.
-Oh, you brute ferocious beasts...-
But why was it that all the cattle,
With bloody eyes, holding their heads high and mighty
Ran to the distant fields,
Fearing the bullets and blazing fire?

Here I am wandering all night long,
     -I am a fool, a pitiful fool-
You deprived me of my brain a long time ago;
Take my life, my Savior, my thoughtless God.

Why are you staring at me, you agonizing eyes?
     -I am a fool, just a fool.-
How envious I am...
You are dying and I am to live this foolish life.
Alone I carried my stupid shadow in the fields of war.
They didn't grant me a single bullet and shouted,
     "He is the fool".

So, listen to me! You that snore with this foolish death,
I will tell you a blazing story, kneaded with blood...
     -I am a fool; a fool I am.-

What pathetic country was it? What year of our Lord?
Who was the king? —Blessed be his soul.
He was really a very fine and a kind king.
I don't know much of the details.
-I even don't even remember his horse's name-
After a nightmare, one day,
The king decreed that in seven cities within seven days

219

All males up to seven years old were to be killed
With the condition not to touch the elderly.
The elderly were so thankful for this decree,
That they offered one of every seven females
As a gift to the king and his comrades...
-A gift of females above the age of seven-
- What a sweet nonsense of the number seven.-

How soon the new kings forgot the old royal wisdom?
Stunned I observe this colossal chaos.
And I ponder. What shall this recreation be called?
Why, I wonder, should these hollow,
Old skulls be severed?
Why bother with these useless lives?
Why crush the bodies that are ready and willing
To bend and serve the king as mules do?
Why expel these humble and tame souls
From the heavens of Arcadia?
They could have spared them at least just one eye,
And they would have prayed for the rest of their lives.
What did the king want from his slaves?
Why kill the already dead?

Why let the orphans live?
Those adoptees of blood and darkness.
The day will come when the masses of those
High-spirited young ones,
Who have nothing at all, nothing anymore,
-Neither parents, nor God, nor a handful of national land-
And who beg for a piece of bread,
Extended to them from afar, in disgust.
Those children did not find sublime traits in

Humans, but only ferocious beasts.
Beware! Those same children, one day,
Will emerge, standing high over
The thousands of decayed bones,
And launch the Bloody Judgment Day.
And they will trumpet to the winds of the world
Their new Will and new Beginning.
And then, behold! Damned will be all living!

"Here we come" -Proclaim those who are coming.
-Don't you hear the stomping of their feet?-
"We, blinded by breathing darkness,
And enraged by the smell of blood.
Here we come... rolling by our shoulders
The centuries-old wheel of our pain
Through the darkness of this globe,
 Over all those who still have a breath to spare.

"Here we come with formidable vigor,
Graced by the granite heels of our Hope,
To make the perished unknowns and the wide-spread
 Cemeteries to speak and shout.

"Here we come! We are the curse!
We are the venomous spear aimed at darkness.
We are the Hydra of vengeance to be caressed,
We are horrified but can cause horrors as well.

"We are the new pilgrims of old vows,
We are the harsh swords and the Book of Laws,
We are the angry waterfall bursting from the mountains,
And the brightness of morning twilight.

To you, who built your wedding tents of sins
And pleasure with our own taut skins,
And to you, idols of worship of Europe,
Who vilely bargained to be silent about our blood.
Shut down the gates of your deaf hearts,
Sharpen your swords, sharpen them secretly.
Sharpen them on your stiff, unmoved conscience,
And the teeth of your children.

"Here we come through the winds,
Don't you hear the whisper of the bones?
We are all sordid corpses, we are all porous skulls
But here we come, here we come..."

***

Let me go, let me rush to cover
This old corpse from the rays of daybreak.
Even the rising sun would be abashed
By the dreadful corpse of the old man
     The dreadful corpse.

Father, you used to say, "The shortest path to heaven
Is to be obedient, to follow the holy path of the Cross."
Father, the shortest path to heaven
Is the dagger of the Kurd,
The dagger of the Kurd!

Wearing shoes of lead, I walk slowly
Over the torsos of thousands of dead.
In reality, my feet grow heavy by the clotted blood.
My feet are heavy.

Lying before me is the flooded river,

I threw him in there... he is floating down the stream.
Farewell, old priest,
The sun will not see you anymore.
No, it will not see you...

Along with thousands before you,
You'll travel down the current; the river is your grave.
Well, farewell, you old brute.
What is the shortest way to heaven, huh?
    Yes, where is the road?

One day, River Sihoon*, on your beautiful centuries-old
Waves, instead of these wicked corpses,
White swans will glide gracefully.
Songs will be sung during evening hours.
    During evening hours...

Sometimes though, maybe only sometimes,
Quietly, from the depths of the river, a skull may appear,
And disrupt the intimate moment of kissing couples...
    That's all... that's all...

There is an infinite reflection of the sky in the water,
-Oh, golden massacre at this moment-
The stars, the Milky Way, the moon and the satellites
Are like a necklace with rolls of pearls,
Grouped in the form of breasts of light,
They pour down the essence of passions.

To die... Stare at the sky... with your bloody eyes,
Poor agonizing souls...
Why can't I cry...? Cry? Oh, No!

But You, You in your unreachable throne,
Brag proudly in the midst of stars.

But You are high, up there and sublime.
Your conscience is clear in your solitude.
You have risen seven times above the seven pearled
Arches, sitting among Your Seraphs,
And don't care to look down with Your unmerciful eyes
At Humanity, which you, yourself spat on this earth.

From the bright steps of Your golden ladder,
Come down Jehovah, Allah, whoever You are.
Beware though!
Turn off your light! Stay in darkness!
This immense place of execution may go mad
And suddenly poke your old eyes with its bloody fingers.

You, miserable fool! Who am I talking to so angrily?
Haven't You been dead for a long time, God?
Your huge corpses, with venomous abomination of blood, has
Polluted the dreams of the pristine Milky Way.

***

The roses have died,
The roses have died.

With their scent and aroma
On their delicate stalks
The roses have died,
The roses have died.

With bloody feet
I tremble as I walk
Barefoot on the corpses.

The roses have died,
The roses have died.

Pity me, oh Lord,
With my hair messy
I walk untimely,
I walk and cry, where is my rose?
Where is my rose?

Oh, how I wish to place
The immense hell in my bosom under his head.
Let my soul die endearingly next to his body...

***

Who is this mournful distressed maiden
In the deep of the night,
Walking endlessly from one corps to the next?
What is that? A sigh?
Who is the fallen in front of whom the poor girl stopped?
A scream...   and the wounded wants to rise. He trembles.
Their arms embrace.
And under the moonlight,
The fallen, in passionate love,
With his bloody, foamy warm mouth,
Agonizing and with a deep sigh,
Touched the rosy lips of the maiden...

What a dreadful scene.
Love reigning in the center of death.
Dark, impassable pathways.

... I shot my gun. The skulls bowed.
I approached them and addressed them loudly-
Hey, friends, Why are you silent?
An abundant hallelujah to you all,
Which is the shortest path to heaven?
Which is it?

***

And then, astounded by their quiet sleep,
I put my head on theirs and stayed still.
My soul went into a deep, deep sleep.

And then a giant tapped on my shoulder and said,
"Hey, madman, tell me, what do you see?"

I spoke to him from the depth of my sleep,
"I see at a distance one hundred towers
Of one hundred ancient cities,
I see lead bullets in the gloomy air,
I see one hundred bells – silenced for ages.
I see one hundred mountains – covered with ashes,
With no pain and no smile – like a desert.
I see fortresses rising by the sides of gorges,
Locked firmly against time.
I see our old tombstones,
Marched upon by a thousand races,
I see one thousand pathways paved with
'Here Lies' epitaphs...
But... look!

All of a sudden, in the darkness of the night
One hundred bells chime in unison,
Piously and consciously,
They shook the dust off of their striking parts.
The silent graves on crossroads,
Pushed open their lids as if in the spirit of a vow,
One hundred princes silently stood up
And are marching majestically in the night...

I see all this and I lament...
It is the procession of the Vow.
The Vow that stills lives beyond Death.
The Vow that crushed the latches of the fortresses
On the mountains...

One hundred princes walk calmly,
Their march carries the weight of seven centuries,
Their shields are rusted, but their eyes are bright,
The chains on their feet hum like a stream.

The weary one who leads the march,
And drags a large muslin cover,
Is that the royal crimson cape?
Or the blood of his race...?
I can't really tell.

Along with and above the procession,
An old bird is groping along,
Is it the royal eagle?
Or the owl of black fate?
I can't really see.

I extended my bloody arms pleading,
-Take me, Oh, take me along,
I want to head to eternity
To the Vow of a race beyond the grave.

But the morning sun is rising,
The one hundred princes descended in unison
From the stony steps of the graves
And everything disappeared... again.
Everything has disappeared again.

Now is the time, where I, like an owl,
Hide secretly In a ditch;
And hide myself from the pristine rays of the sun...

- *Sihoon- Seyhan-* a river flowing through Adana, Turkey.

THE DEATH OF A POET

I set out on a voyage early at dawn before sunrise.
I was walking crushing roses and mints in the fields.
Motionless were the flowers as if God was asleep in them.

Only a brook was weeping under the bushes.
Flowing down the stream, on its foamy waves,
It was carrying a pale teenager.

He had lilacs in his hand and was taking them to Erato.
The flowers on the banks of the brook
Were wishing him safe journey, saying, "Good bye, good bye."

Alas, I recognized the boy in the brook,
It was my shadow.
I wanted to escape, but could not.
 -One cannot run away from himself-

That death is within me; I am that boy!
I have shut closed the gates of sunrise
For I know darkness is imminent.

Before my budding flowers wither,
I carry my tear-filled songs,
Coming to the big Sea, Almighty God.

(Written on March 7, 1911)

GENERAL REFERENCES

ALBOAYADJIAN, ARSHAG, "Krikor Zohrab" in *Anhedatsogh Temker (*Disappearing Figures), Constantinople, 1919.

ANDONIAN, ARAM, *Ayn Sev Orerun* (During Those Dark Days), Boston, 1919.

ANDONIAN, ARAM, The Memoirs of Naim Bey, London, 1920.

ASADOOR, HRAND, *Timasdverner* (Shadows of Figures), Constantinople, 1919.

BALAKIAN, BISHOP KRIKORIS, *Hay Koghkotan* (Armenian Golgotha), Vienna, 1922.

BRYCE JAMES, IST VISCOUNT, The Treatment of Armenians in the Ottoman Empire. Compiled by Arnold J. Toynbee. 1916 [Documents presented to Viscount Grey of Fallodon, Secretary of State for Foreign Affairs]]

CHOBANIAN, ARSHAG, "Memories" in *Anahid,* No. 3, Paris, 1930.

CHOBANIAN, ARSHAG, *Tlgadintsin yev ir Kordsuh* (Tlgadintsi and his Works), Boston, 1927.

DADRIAN, VAHAKN, The History of the Armenian Genocide, Oxford, 1997.

DAVIS, LESLIE A., The Slaughterhouse Province An American Diplomat's Report on the Armenian Genocide of 1915-1917, Susan K. Blair, Ed., New York, 1988.

DEMIRJYAN BEDROSS, *Vark Indrayi* (Indra's life), Yerevan, 2003.

GARABEDIAN, L., *Tulgadintsin* (Tlgadintsi), Yerevan, 1996.

GUST, WOLFGANG, The Armenian Genocide, Oxford, 2014.

HACIKYAN, AGOP; BASMAJIAN, GABRIEL; FRANCHUK, EDWARD; OUZOUNIAN, NOURHAN, The Heritage of Armenian Literature, Vol. 3, Detroit, 2000.

HAYGAGAN SOVEDAGAN HANRAKIDARAN (Armenian Soviet Encyclopedia" Vol. 1-12, Yerevan, 1979.

HOVAKIMIAN, BAKHTIYAR, *Yeghernuh Hay Taderagan Arvesti mech* (The Genocide in Armenian Theatrical Literature), Yerevan, 2000.

HOVAKIMYAN, BAKHTIAR, *Dsadsganoonneri Parraran* (The Dictionary of Pennames),Yerevan, 2005.

HOVANNISIAN, RICHARD, G., Editor, The Armenian People Vol. 1 and. 2, New York, 1997.

HOVANNISIAN, RICHARD, G, Editor, Remembrance and Denial, Detroit, 1998.

HYOOSIAN, M., *Krikor Zohrabi Arvesduh* (Krikor Zohrab's Art), Yerevan, 1964.

HYOOSIAN, M., Krikor Zohrab, Vol. V, 1957, Beirut.

ISHKHAN, MOUSHEGH, *Hay Kraganootyoon* (Armenian Literature) Vol. 1, Vol. 2, 1982, Vol. 3, Beirut, 2001.

JANASHIAN, M., *Badmootyoon Arti Hay Kraganootyan* (History of Modern Armenian Literature) Vol. I, Venice, 1953.

NAHADAG KRAKEDNEROO PAREGAMNER (Friends of Martyred Writers) Vol 1 through Vol. 7, Paris, 1930s.

OSHAGAN, HAGOP, *Hay Kraganootyoon* (Armenian Literature) 3rd printing, Jerusalem, 1966.

OSHAGAN, HAGOP, *Hamaynabadger Arevmdahay Kraganootyan* (An Overview of Western Armenian Literature), Jerusalem, 1945.

SEVAG, ROOPEN, *Garmir Kirkuh* (The Red Book), Constantinople, 1909.

SEVAG, ROOPEN, *Yerger* (Literary Works), Beirut, 1986.

SEVAG, ROOPEN, *Yerger* {Collective works), Yerevan, 1995.

SHAHPAZ, *Krikor Zohrab* (Krikor Zohrab), Beirut, 1959.

SMPAD PURAD, *Yerger* (Literary Works), Yerevan, 2001.

TAMRAZIAN, HRANT, *Siamanto* (Siamanto), Yerevan, 2003.

TEKMEZIAN, ASDGHIG, *Arevmdahay Kraganootyan Undrani*, (Selections from Western Armenian Literature), Yerevan. 1999.

TEOTIG, *Hooshartsan Abril 11* (Memorial Monument- April 11, 1919, Constantinople. [Published for the commemorative event of 1919 in Constantinople. The booklet lists 783 names of martyred writers, political activists, and religious and community leaders. This booklet is one of the most important documentation about the Armenian Genocide.]

TOLOLIAN, MINAS, *Tar muh Kraganootyoon* (A Century of Armenian Literature), Second Printing, Vol. 1, Boston, 1977.

VAROOZHAN, TANIEL, *Panasdeghdsagan Yerger* (Poetic Works), Beirut, 1986.

FTRANSLITERATION FOR WESTERN ARMENIAN DIALECT

The English letters not mentioned here are pronounced in their accepted usage.

English Letter	Pronunciation
a	As "a" in mart
ch	A "ch" in church.
e	As "e" in met
g	As "g" in girl
h	As "h" in hat
	At the end of the letter "u" as in huh
I	As "i" in sit (short ee sound)
o	As "o" in sort
oo	As "oo" in mood
rr	As "r" in the Italian pronunciation of bravo.
u	As "u" in but
y	As "y" in yard
ts	As "ts" in parts
dz	As "dz" in Godzilla
zh	As "s" in pleasure

DR. HERAND M. MARKARIAN

A scientist, professor, playwright, poet, director, actor, literary and theater critic, and translator, he was born in Basrah, Iraq in 1938.

He holds B.Sc., M.S. and Ph.D. degrees in Chemistry and an M.S. in Management of Technology. Along with his scientific studies, he studied playwriting and directing at the Circle in the Square, Schreiber Studio, and NYU's Tisch School for the Arts in NYC.

He first appeared on the stage in 1956 in his birthplace of Basrah, in the role of the Poet in H. Baronian's play, the Gentlemen Beggars. His first poem was published in 1957 in Koyamard Weekly in Baghdad, Iraq. His directing debut was in 1958 in Baghdad, Iraq.

He has adapted for the stage the works of H. Toomanian, R. Sevag, B. Sevag, H. Baronian, Hamasdegh, A. Arpine, J. Hagopian, A. Giragossian, H. Shiraz, M. Tololian, R. Hovhannessian, N. Shnorhali, T. Varoozhan, and H. Markarian.

He has authored 26 plays, a book of poems and a travelogue; he has published 13 books, directed 53 plays, and acted in more than 50 plays. He also edited the works of 13 Armenian playwrights. Markarian founded the NY and NJ Hamazkayin Theater Groups. He edited Varak periodical for ten years and is currently on the Editorial Board of Pakine Literary periodical. He has been a professor in the SUNY system for 10 years and lectured at the Siamanto Academy of the Eastern Prelacy of the Armenian Church for 25 years. He is an adjunct professor at St. Nersess Armenian Seminary of the Eastern Diocese of the Armenian Church and has lectured extensively in the USA, Canada, England, France, Greece, Lebanon, Syria, Iraq, Armenia, and Artsakh. He has presented numerous multi-media productions.

His plays have been presented in the USA, Canada, Armenia, Syria, Lebanon, Greece, and England. He had two successful theatrical performance runs Off-Broadway in NYC in 1995 and 2012.

AUTHORSHIP OF PLAYS

Shurchanuh (The Cycle)	1971
Soghomon Tehlirian	1975
Peverrneruh (Polarization)	1977
Vartanank	1979
Verzhin	1980
Potorig Kavati muh mech	1980
(A tempest in a cup)	
Ayt Anoosh Lezood Oodem	1980
(I Love Your Utterance)	
Aghotkis Mi Kharnvir	1981
(Don't Pry in My Prayers)	
Merrnil Chkidsogh Antsyaluh	1982
(The Everlasting Past)	
Gyank muh hink vargyani mech	1982
(A Life in Five Minutes)	
Horizonnerern Hrgizvads	1984
(From Horizons Ablazed)	
Yes Asdgheruh Goozem Krgel	1987
(Embracing the Stars)	
Hayrig Looysi Arrakyaluh	1988
(Hayrig, the Apostle of Light)	
Ooghevoruh (The Voyager)	1990
Yev Yerginken Yerek Atorr Ingav	
(And Three Chairs Fell from Heaven)	1991
Al Zhoghovi Chem Yertar	1992
(No More Meetings)	
Hetoom Arka (King Hetoom)	1993
Asdvadsneruh Pobig En	1993

(Gods Are Barefoot)
Mirrors (Eng.)   1993
Domsag muh Door Tadron Gertam   1994
   (Give me a Free Ticket and I'll Attend Theater)
Vazem Chooshanam   1997
   (Run Don't be Late)
Navabdooyduh (The Cruise)   2003
Yerp Arevuh gu Lrre   2005
   (When the Sun is Silenced)
The Georgetown Boys (Bilingual)   2007
Silence in a Circular Rainbow (Eng.)   2009
Testimonies   2014

POETRY
Yentayessen Pshrvads   2000
   (From the Shattered Inner World)

SENTIMENTAL TRAVELOGUE
Liturgy, Sound of Stones   1998

PUBLICATIONS
Vartanank   1979
Soghomon Tehlirian   1980
The Cycle (Pakine Periodical)   1988
Mirrors (Eng.)   1996
King Hetoom (Pakine Periodical)   2000
Run Don't be Late (Pakine Periodical)   2002
The Voyager   2004
When the Sun is Silenced   2005
And Three Chairs Fell from Heaven
   (Dramaturgia Periodical)   2008
Mirrors (Arm.)   2011
Zahrad 90 (Eng.)   2014

TRANSLATIONS (Armenian to English)- Antigone, Jean Anouilh with J. Markarian. V. Tekeyan, H. Toomanian, K. Khodigian's plays, Zahrad's poems, H. M. Markarian, Hrant, Tlgadintsi, Zohrab, Purad, Yeroukhan, Zartarian, Haroutunian, Siamanto, Parseghian, Varoozhan, Chogurian, Sevag,

AWARDS AND CITATIONS

1980   The Gold Medal, Hamazkayin USA and Canada

1980   Honorary Member- ARS Mayr Chapter, NY.

1987   St. Mesrob Mashdots Medal. His Holiness Karekin Sarkissian, the Great House of Cilicia.

1992   Best Diaspora Playwright, the Writers' Union of Armenia, Yerevan, Armenia.

1992   Membership- Writers' Union of Armenia, Yerevan, Armenia.

2002   Gold Medal, Minister of Culture of Armenia, Armenia.

2002   Cultural Achievements, Claire Schulman, Borough President of Queens, NY

2004   The Vahrich and Verzhin Jebejian Playwright Award, Beirut, Lebanon.

2008   Agnoony Award, ARS Eastern Region, MA, USA.

2008   Hagop Meghabard Award, National Library of Armenia.

2009   Hamazkayin Medal of Honor, Hamazkayin Central Executive.

2010   Artavazd Award, the Theater Society of Armenia.

2010   Cultural Achievement Medal, Jersey City, NJ

2012   Movses Khorenatsi Medal Serge Sarkissian, President, Armenia

2013   Voice of Armenia TV, North Bergen, NJ, USA

2014   Service Award- Hamazkayin Central Executive

Markarian in "The Ethnic Theater in the United States," Parlakian, N. p 19, 1983 M.S. Seller, Ed.

"Mirrors" was reprinted in "Contemporary American Armenian Playwrights*" by N. Parlakian. Columbia U. Press pp233, 2004*

INDEX

THE MARTYRED ARMENIAN WRITERS

1915 -1922

-An Anthology-

Herand M. Markarian

ACKNOLEDGMENT AND SINCERE THANKS TO

Iris Chekenian

George Dermksian, M.D.

Janet Mouradian, M.D.

Gahmk S. Markarian, J.D.

Yeraz N. Markarian Meschian, Ph. D.

For reviewing
the different parts of the manuscript and making most
valuable suggestions.

COVER PHOTOGRAPHY, PHOTO COMPOSITION AND DESIGN

Neshan Koulian

PICTURE EDITING

Armen Meschian and Vartavarr Keshishian

PUBLICATION

LIBRA-6 PRODUCTIONS, INC.

160 Waters Edge, Congers, NY

ISBN 978-0-692-34476-7

2015

EPILOGUE

A CANDLE LIT

A candle lit will not shatter the darkness abound.
May not suffice to mourn or cry,
Lament the dead and perished folk.

A candle lit is too feeble to scream sorrow,
Trumpet loud for justice lost.

A candle lit is not some goods to be traded,
*   -   It is not gold, silver or oil, nor a ruby or a prized jewel-*

A candle lit stands alone on window sills
Burns endlessly
*   In loneliness*
*   And hopelessness...*

***

But if you have that lit candle
Deep in the folds of your brave soul,
Then its feeble, flickering light,
Becomes a sun —unbound and pure-

Then the Martyrs will come smiling
Row upon row of young and old.

For the candles they lit before,
*   -   Before they faced their gloomy demise-*
Now are shining deep in your soul.

***

Light a candle for you and me!

Herand M. Markarian

CPSIA information can be obtained at www.ICGtesting.com
Printed in the USA
BVOW04s2007230315

392941BV00003BA/9/P